THE RIVER WITHIN

THE RIVER WITHIN

A Life of Fly Fishing

WILLIAM B. CURRIE

MERLIN UNWIN BOOKS

Published by Merlin Unwin Books, 21 Corve Street, Ludlow, Shropshire, England

ISBN 1-873674-10-4

MERLIN UNWIN BOOKS
21 Corve Street, Ludlow
Shropshire SY8 1DA

Typeset in Bembo 11 on 12 point by BMD Graphics, Hemel Hempstead.
Printed and bound in Great Britain by Butler & Tanner Ltd, Frome and London.

Designed by John Leath MSTD.

I do not know much about gods; but I think that the river
Is a strong brown god – sullen, untamed and intractable,
. . .

His rhythm was present in the nursery bedroom,
In the rank ailanthus of the April dooryard,
In the smell of grapes on the autumn table,
And the evening circle in the winter gaslight.
The river is within us . . .

T. S. ELIOT

When (feelings of delight) are past, it is almost as impossible to give an account of them as it is of 'last year's
clouds', and the attempt to analyse and reconstruct the
sense of joy that has been and may be again seems to result
in rows of dead words.

GREY OF FALLODON, *Fly Fishing* (1899)

Contents

Introduction

G‍REY OF FALLODON, a statesman, a countryman, an ardent trout
and salmon fisher and a much loved angling author, said that writing
about a day's fishing, no matter how skilfully, always meant that the
half had not been told. It was not, he argued, that there was nothing to
tell; it was 'because of the nature of joy'. Language was better suited to
argument and thought, he believed, than to feeling. Feelings of delight,
like those he found in fishing, 'come unsought and without effort...
like an atmosphere'. He wrote:

> When (feelings of delight) are past, it is almost as impossible to give
> an account of them as it is of 'last year's clouds', and the attempt to
> analyse and reconstruct the sense of joy that has been and may be
> again seems to result in rows of dead words. *Fly Fishing*, 1899, p.4

Anyone who has read *Fly Fishing* knows that it is a book very far
indeed from dead words. It is evocative, inspirational and full of joy.
Yet fishing, which every fisherman knows is a whole realm of delight,
has, in the last fifty years, produced a mass of writing, most of which is
instructional, factual and discursive. I know. I have been part of it.
There is, of course, a great pleasure in talking shop, of rivers and pools,
rods and reels, tactics and fish. It is true that in even the most factual
descriptions of a fishing day our deeper delight can shine through. I
know, however, that Grey is right; the half has not been told.

It is almost as if Grey was pointing out that fishing has right-hand
and left-hand dimensions, the former concerned with skills and the
latter with insights and feelings. But how are we to bring out the feelings – the untold half? For me, as I hope this book shows, fishing
funnels you into its skills and its delights through apparently obvious

9

things – rivers and fish, tackle, weather and all the layered experiences of days spent on the water. Fishing days and fishing places themselves provide the soil in which the pleasure grows. *The River Within* is thus a book about going fishing, about rivers, their fish, about growing under their influence, being obsessed by them and delighting in them.

Writing about fishing waters is, I realise, also writing about my life. Some rivers, especially those first fished in my boyhood, have a deep personal place in my feelings; others have a much more practical signi-ficance, linked with different kinds of fishing, perhaps associated with a time of year, or even, as for instance in the case of sea trout fishing, with times of day or night. The book is about the landscapes I love. As you would expect, many of the waters in this book are in my own country, Scotland; others are in more exotic places which I have been lucky enough to travel to. *The River Within*, therefore, is not a *vade mecum*, although we cannot talk or write about fishing without some sharing of experience, and therefore learning taking place. Nor is it a guide book except in the deeper sense that it invites readers to come with me to some of the places my fishing has taken me to and to share not only the sport but also perhaps something of the feelings of delight fishing has produced.

I share the urge to go fishing with countless others. It is one of the most widely known and happily shared compulsions of mankind. If you were to ask me to explain it, I would try to avoid wearing the rather stark spectacles of the anthropologist who would see fishing as a kind of hangover from the hunter–gatherer side of primitive man. I am also wary of other explanations, for example, those which label fishing as recreational, or describe it as a leisure pursuit. There are elements in the word 'leisure' which distinctly demean the art of angling. Fishing is undoubtedly an antidote to urbanism and a relief from the pressures of work, but it is much more. For example, it is always associated in some way with travel and with some aspect of the wilderness, or the sea or the solitary place. A wonderful feature of the sport is that even a visit to the local reservoir on a Wednesday afternoon somehow taps into this rich spring. Fishing is a marvellous field of human activity, both physical and spiritual. It abounds with vivid images – of natural beauty, wildness, unspoiled nature, mystery, story and myth. Its literature is enormous. It is biblical, classical and romantic, as well as technical and discursive. Fishing literature offers a profusion of narratives, is rich in allusion, reflection and self-awareness. It has enriched the language of fishers and non-fishers alike with an abundance of images which are fundamental to human experience.

What can we say, then, about this extraordinary force which makes us want to fish and produces so much delight in its *aficionados*? If you hold up a glass and look closely at fishing, will you see what fishers do, feel, hope and believe? You will certainly see people and places; a host of fishing waters gracing the land; a great resource of fish in a natural environment and fishers well aware of the need to cherish and care for it. Perhaps deeper, you will savour the paradox that wilderness and paradise are the same place. You might find that the fishers were paradoxical too, for, while they passionately pursue the fish to catch them, they are also deeply committed to their care. But in any glass we look through, with a comparatively small, often unnoticed, shift of focus, what we see is ourselves. Fishing is an important part of our personal history and of self-knowledge; it is one of the metaphors interpreting our lives.

There is a naivety in it too. I feel myself, when I am fishing, rather like Mole in Kenneth Grahame's *The Wind in the Willows*:

> By the side of the river he trotted as one trots, when very small, by
> the side of a man who holds one spellbound by exciting stories; and
> when tired at last, he sat on the bank, while the river still chattered
> on to him, a babbling procession of the best stories in the world,
> sent from the heart of the earth to be told at last to the insatiable sea.

The River Within, therefore, is a book about layers of things, beginning with the delights of fishing waters and the country they take us into. My hope is that the reader will share my journeys to rivers, my fishing in them and my thoughts about them. I hope I may in some small measure, in writing about this passionate world, have gone beyond 'rows of dead words' and have been able to say something about joy. For fishers, of course, as I am sure Grey knew, joy is quite simply reached through the actual experience of going fishing. It is my belief that we are immensely privileged, because, in our sport, practicality and imagination are wedded to each other; adventure and contemplation go hand in hand.

CHAPTER
I

In the Strath of Kildonan

I WAS EIGHT when I first set eyes on the Helmsdale during the course of a family picnic and it is not pitching it too high to say that it overwhelmed me. We were half way through our regular holiday in Caithness, where my father's closest friend, Henry, farmed. He was a fellow Scots Guardsman and my father and he had spent four years together, much of it in the trenches during the First World War and both had, miraculously, survived. A picnic was planned. We drove down from Caithness over the Berriedale river, stopping to lean over the old bridge and see what seemed to me to be scores of grey shapes, the backs of salmon waiting for water to run the river. We climbed the dangerous hill on the road south of Berriedale and rolled down to Helmsdale. Then, turning west into the Strath of Kildonan, we drove up the river valley, past Kildonan itself to Suisgill Lodge where we sat by the river and talked and had lunch and, in the company of an old man whose name I cannot remember, I walked by the river. He kept saying he was itching to fish there. The Helmsdale was, on that August day, ringed with the rises of trout and parr and here and there, most dramatically, salmon splashed. There were gardens to visit, but the old man and I did not go to them. We were possessed by the river. We walked up to the Wood Pool, then down again to what I remember most vividly, the long glide in front of Suisgill Lodge, the far bank lined with small trees, the water brown with peat from the moors above. It was a magical sight. I might have hoped then that I would come back to the Helmsdale and fish it, for I had already begun my fishing career, and had earlier that summer caught a trout on the fly in the Stinchar in Ayrshire. I wonder if I knew intuitively then that the Helmsdale was to become a water I was to fish regularly and come to know and love.

That was the late summer of 1938 and the month was August. My
parents and Henry and his sister sat on the grass and talked while my
sister and brother played on the sward. I cannot recall all the adults
discussed, but I know that the burden of their conversation was the
threat of war in Europe. You might have expected Henry and my
father, in talking about a coming war, to refer to their experiences in a
former one, but rather significantly, then and at all other times, they
avoided speaking about the Great War, except in a very general way. It
was as if the actual horror of the war was too gross to articulate. My
father and Henry seemed to have boxed the four war-years away,
to have interred them, with all their horrors, and staunchly refused to
exhume what they had buried. In my bloodthirsty early teens during
the Second World War, I sometimes pressed my father for stories of the
trenches, but he never gave me any details. I attribute to the trenches,
however, the bonds which my father and Henry shared. They demon-
strated a closeness of the deepest sort, an immovable locking together
of two lives. As a child I was continually impressed by their depth of
understanding and love for each other. Both men were deeply religious
and were convinced of divine help in the war. Once, in response to one
of my questions about his survival, my father answered me and ended
the conversation with one three-word utterance. 'We were preserved,'
he said.

I saw the Helmsdale after that out of the train window, tantalisingly,
en route for Caithness from 1945 onwards, but I had no chance to fish it
then. I devoured my home rivers, the Ayr, the Doon, the Girvan and
the lochs in the Ayrshire hills. I grew into the Tay and Spey and a host
of Highland waters. I explored waters overseas. but I did not get the
chance to fish the Helmsdale until a friend invited me to join him on the
river in March 1976. I felt very welcome. I had a fish on my first day,
out of the Manse pool on lower beat six. Since then I have fished the
river regularly every spring, usually in the last week of February or
early March, with the very occasional invitation to fish a day during the
summer. It is still for me a place of marvellous individuality, of
solitude and promise, all the more attractive because many years
separated my boyhood dream of fishing it and actually experiencing it
as a salmon water. More than any water I know, the Helmsdale is an
alluring river. Its salmon fishing is, of course excellent, but its atmosphere is inscrutable and the Strath of Kildonan through which it
reaches the sea is one of the most serene glens known to me in
Scotland.

It is the lower river that I know best, since I fish mostly in the spring
and the lower six beats, below the falls of Kildonan, provide all
the fishing up to April. But the river, brown from its tributaries in the
moors above, links its lower waters in the strath with the heather and

lochs of Badanloch Forest – not a forest at all, but an open Sutherland moor with excellent trout fishing. Walking north up the Garvault Burn above the Badanloch, for example, you can fish Coire na Mang, a small, almost circular loch with clear water, or cross the short hill ridge between this loch and Druim a' Cliabhain (usually pronounced Drum na Claiven) or, if you walk a mile or so further north you will reach Loch Crocach. Coire na Mang has for long had the reputation for producing good-sized trout, even if in recent seasons it has failed to do so. I was fishing it one July day with my son and, in true Sutherland style, I put on a large dropper fly, a big Black Pennell which scurried around on the surface like a dapping fly. In the middle of a drift a large black head appeared, almost casually engulfed the fly and snapped it off. It was all over in a couple of seconds, and with the plucking off of the bob fly went my chance to take one of the Coire na Mang monsters, which would no doubt have dwarfed the good trout of a pound-and-a-half I took shortly afterwards.

That same day I walked over to Drum (a' Cliabhain) and fished it from the bank and while I was looking out over the loch I had a rare sight; I saw a salmon lunge clear out of the water. Not many fish reach this remote loch. That salmon must have run the Helmsdale, over the Falls of Kildonan, up the Private river (Strath Beg/Bannock Burn on the map), up the little Claggan Burn to Loch Arichlinie, up the even smaller burn above, which flows for at least three miles through the heather on the north-eastern side of Ben Griam More and rises 350 feet into Drum. The journey of that salmon to Drum is a kind of mini-version of the whole Helmsdale saga, of fish from the North Sea running the river and twenty miles inland meeting the moors with their multiple burns and lochs where they can lose themselves in the wildness. Drum is, on that side of the strath, as far as a salmon can go. I did look at the tiny burn between Drum and Coire na Mang, and I wondered whether it might *just* be possible in a wet year for a salmon to reach that round loch with its big, dropper-snapping trout. That would be the absolute limit, even in imagination, for beyond that there is only the moss itself and one tiny tributary running steeply down from Ben Griam More.

The main Lochs at the top of the Helmsdale are all on the Badanloch Estate and they include the Badanloch itself, a large, deep water which has been dammed to form a reservoir for the Helmsdale below. Water flow can be regulated there, and in summer all twenty-five miles of the river can be kept fishable in periods of low rainfall or drought. The salmon, especially the spring fish, enter the Badanloch, and past the island, run into Loch nan Clar above. From there they can travel further, going through the narrows and into Loch Rimsdale to the west. There is one further possible step, but I do not know if it is ever

taken. Salmon might negotiate the Truderscaig Burn out of Rimsdale
and reach the loch above. That lovely, shallow moorland trout loch
with its feeder burns is the westernmost extent of the Helmsdale
system. At one point Loch Truderscaig is only a mile over the moor
from the Mallart River, which feeds the Naver and drains north from
the watershed to join the Pentland Firth, while the Helmsdale flows east
to the North Sea. In July 1986, when I was fishing with a party from
Loch Choire Lodge, I spent the morning and most of the afternoon
fishing Truderscaig for trout and we had a good catch, and barbecued
some of the morning's trout in the shelter of the ruined boathouse
there. I had a romantic notion. I thought I would like to walk across the
mile or so of moor from the loch to the Mallart river and, if luck was
with me, take a salmon from one of its pools, linking, as it were,
Helmsdale water with that of the Naver. The way lay over a rutted
moor with a small plantation of trees to the north, then winding among
its open banks I discovered the Mallart. It was low, but had salmon in
its deeper pools. Fishing my trout rod and using that unusual technique
which I have found only on the Mallart, I stalked salmon and drew a
tiny oiled tube over their lies under the turf and reed banks. I had to
crawl like an Indian scout to reach the salmon undisturbed. Two fish
moved to my fly. One turned away an inch from the little tube as it was
drawn off the glassy water, leaving a little wake. Another came more
quickly and plucked the small tube hard, as if frightened by its own
boldness. It was on for a matter of seconds only, and was my last offer
of the afternoon.

As a salmon fisher, my detailed knowledge of the Helmsdale river
only extends from the falls of Kildonan to the sea, since my fishings are
normally in the early spring before fish generally pass over the falls and
populate the upper river. The Kildonan Falls, which mark the great
divide between the moorland Helmsdale and the faster lower river, are
impressive and I always pause on the wire suspension bridge which
spans the gorge immediately below. Sometimes I see a fish running,
even as early as February – bad news because it means we are losing the
stock of the lower river. More often I just gaze at the pounding water,
and make my mind boggle at the astronomical number of salmon
which must have run them, even in my lifetime. I was there fishing
beat six in late February recently crossing in heavy rain to fish the river
from the right bank. I returned to the falls a couple of hours later to
find that the succession of heavy north-western showers was raising the
river very rapidly. It was impressive. I stopped on the wire bridge and
saw the falls progressively changing colour as the flood rose. As I
watched, the sound amplified and the normal roar became a thunder;
the shape of the falls and the gorge and all the pools below altered as the
spate surged, filling and flattening out and concealing the many neuks

and lies below. The little suspension bridge began to vibrate in the full orchestration of the storm – a gale of wind from the north west, the pounding roar of the falls and the hiss of bursts of lashing rain. It out-Wagnered Wagner! The thrill of it out there was immense. I stood in the middle of the swinging bridge, exhilarated by the tumult, and clung on, feeling brave. I was all set to revel in it, but as the water rose and the wind blew harder, my courage turned to awe, then to anxiety. The suspension bridge rocked and jigged and suddenly seemed flimsy. It flashed through my mind that a much more elaborate bridge, built by the army at Kilearnan further downstream, collapsed in its first storm and had to be rebuilt. I decided to cut short the thrill of hanging on to the wires in the middle of the bridge above the maelstrom and, clutching my salmon rod and hauling myself along by the wires, I crept cautiously off it, conscious now of apprehension and fear. Being a voyeur is very different from being a participant. The spectacle of the Kildonan falls rising fast in flood, which had at first thrilled me, now chastened me and filled me with dread.

I have taken fish from the falls pool in spring, but have never had the problem of salmon leaving the pool and running down the gorge, through McCormack's below and the Flats below that, although this has happened to numerous anglers. I think about it though. I fantasise, and imagine the route I would take and how I would put my foot on this rock and that, would drop down the bank here, and gain line on him here and give line there. I would, probably, land him at the tail of the deep chasm called The Flats. But if a fish went further than the Flats … Ah!… that would be some adventure, because there is rough water and a fall below there and on the left bank of the river sits the Big Rock, an enormous boulder which you can reach by way of a light wire-suspension bridge. Fantasy sometimes takes me further and I play the fish after climbing with impressive agility on to the big rock. In a decade-and-a-half of fishing there, although I have hooked fish in both the Falls Pool and the Flats, none has given me the chance to turn my fantasy into fact. There are numerous tales of this actually happening, but a fish running hard down broken water with falls, and taking to pools on the other side of rocks large enough to need bridges to get to, seems to have all the odds of nature on its side.

I did have something similar however, when I was standing at the downstream end of that same Big Rock. Below it is a fine glide, memorably but inexplicably named the Vale of Tears. I think of it more as the Vale of Smiles. It is one of the most exciting and productive casts on beat six. The Big Rock pool is very deep and holds a large number of salmon in virtually complete safety. They splash in there, or show head-and-tail under the overhanging cliff on the right bank and from this holding pool, they tail back to lie in the Vale of Tears below.

Standing on the tip of the Big Rock, with the deep backwater below, you can put a fly beautifully over the Vee of the Vale of Tears where the waters of the river concentrate and suck out of the Big Rock pool above to make a deep, glassy glide between shingle on the right and rocks and grass on the left bank.

I was fishing with George Hardy, the Achentoul ghillie, in one of my first days on beat six and I was in a talkative mood. I was asking him whether you normally saw takes in the Vale when you were fishing a big sunk fly for spring salmon. My inch-and-three-quarters waddington fished on a medium-sink line was not visible in the brown glide as I fished it across, despite its being a prominent and large fly. I had embellished it myself. I had been sharpening the treble hook on it in preparation for the Helmsdale (in the days when waddingtons did not have changeable trebles and points had to be kept sharp) and, for some whim, I tied on some straggling yellow and red hair to the sparse original dressing. George was, I think, replying to my question about seeing fish take, when the Vale of Tears suddenly bulged and a roundel of black waves erupted over its surface. The line pulled and he was on, as if the salmon had heard my question to George and wanted to answer it for itself. George said something in a choked voice which sounded like, 'My God Bill! *That's* a fish!'. I said nothing, I was hanging on to the rod on the tip of the Big Rock, hoping that I had made a good job of sharpening the hooks of the fly. The salmon at first seemed obliging, and ran up towards me out of the Vale and into the Big Rock pool beside us where, almost under the rod point, it toured round twice as if inspecting the place. Then, with massive decision, it turned and ran downstream and my reel made a long, sustained, anxious sound. George was shouting something about following him and, without needing much of a prompt, I plunged into the brown water off the tip of the rock and was relieved to find a sandy bottom waist deep or a little more and I barged through it, clambering up on to the grass beyond and, in a stumbling run, I began to get some line back. But the fish, having got to the Vale of Tears again, decided to go further. It turned and sped down through the rough water below, into the Little Rock stream below that, taking more backing out, and there it paused for long enough for me to run down the bank and win some of the backing back on to the reel again. Would the salmon now stop in the Little Rock and behave normally? No, it would not. It was a big, powerful fish and after some adventures in the Little Rock it surged down through the two sections of that pool and continued down the streamy water below. By now I was on a decent bank and could follow easily. I was puffing and blowing a little, but so was the salmon. He hung in under the far bank, but I managed to hold on to him and keep the pressure up and the salmon began to respond in a more orthodox way, and showed that it was tiring. It turned downstream again, but this time I was able to steer it a bit and when it stopped near a single oak tree not far above the head of the Manse Pool below, I brought it in. After a circle or two and one heart-stopping difficulty when the net was first put in, we managed to land it. It was a cock fish, eighteen-and-a-half pounds, and, like many fish of this size, had seemed more powerful than its weight merited. It had taken us through three pools, about 250 or 300 yards downstream. It had taken me at full pelt through an uncharted backwater, which I have looked at again and again since, and I can vouch for the fact that for the last ten years it has been deep enough to drown you. I don't think I walked on water when I followed the fish through it. But it is curious. Sandbanks come and go on the Helmsdale annually. Did the river benevolently spin a bridge for me? Was that occasion the one and only year when that backwater could have been waded?

I love beat six, the Falls, the Gorge, the two Rocks and the long Manse Pool with its Swirlies near the tail. Below that, the Church Stream runs beside the small Kildonan church, standing right down by the river, with its cemetery of headstones beside, many old, but with a scattering of new ones in an extension built out into the field. Some find it odd that there is a church there without any visible community to serve. What congregation filled the remote Kildonan church down by the river? The answer is that from the late eighteenth century, and well into the nineteenth century, the Strath of Kildonan, like many other Highland straths and the islands of the Hebrides, suffered one of the most painful and radical movements of population in Scottish history; the Strath was cleared of its people by the landlords. It may be hard for us in the twentieth century to grasp that what is now a virtually empty valley was seriously overpopulated in the eighteenth century. The people largely lived by subsistence farming, but by constant sub-division, the holdings had become too small. The poverty of this life of subsistence was severe. Many people moved voluntarily to the south in the eighteenth century, and some met a worse form of poverty in Glasgow. Some were forced to move to other parts of Sutherland, as, for example, the 2000 luckless families moved to the unbroken lands of Eriboll where they experienced the most terrible privations. Others decided to emigrate to America and Canada, but many refused to leave their homes and the lairds, intent on agricultural improvements, through their factors, forced them to leave by legal and illegal methods – and by evictions, some of which included burning the houses down, they cleared the Kildonan people from the strath.

Looking back, it is clear that a radical change of agriculture and a radical redistribution of population was necessary, but that does not justify the brutality which the landowners sometimes applied. The

church at Kildonan, with its small windows still looking out over
the river, witnessed this, and I can detect its unease as I fish down the
Church Stream by its side. If you leave the pool and walk round
the building, you will see an interesting plaque set into the east wall.

In memory of George Bannerman of Kildonan,
great-grandfather of the Right Honourable
John G. Diefenbaker PC, QC, MP,
Prime Minister of Canada 1957–1963,
and of all the Selkirk Settlers from Kildonan
who, in 1812 and 1813 migrated to the Red
River Settlement, in what is now the Province of
Manitoba.

One distinguished grandson returning to pay homage to his forebears
does not make an argument for the clearances. There is no plaque on
the walls of Kildonan to remind us of the innumerable folk for whom
clearance from the Strath of Kildonan led to misery and death.

I am conscious of layer upon layer of human history when I am
fishing the Helmsdale, and I am very aware that I am a vitually anony-
mous atom in the current veneer. I walk down the banks of the wind-
swept beat five and stumble over grassy mounds covering the ruins of
former cottages. I see them again on beats four and three, dead hamlets.
Beside them in places, all down the valley, are much older ruins, stone-
age sites, hut circles and the cell of at least one saint. The river flows
on, giving the illusion of being permanent, while successive civilisa-
tions, including our own, establish themselves, then decline and, save
for the mounds of grassy stones, disappear.

In a sense the Helmsdale today is anachronistic. It has suffered less
than many Highland valleys dependent on sporting estates. The reason
for this is the river with its marvellous crop of salmon. In a normal year
the Helmsdale will produce for the six estates owning it, a grand total
of 2500 salmon or more. The fishery is managed as a single unit, with all
the estates taking part in a daily rotation of beats allowing rods in the
course of one week to have access to the whole river. There is an agreed
estuary netting policy, a re-stocking policy for the whole river, water
levels management and effective bailiffing. The result is that the river,
far more than the stalking or the grouse shooting or the farming is the
key to the continuity of the Strath in its modern form. The Helmsdale
has, I believe, a message for other Scottish fisheries – that rivers are best
managed as whole coherent units with agreed objectives. Having only

six proprietors helps. A proposition is in its most effective form when it has the smallest possible number of parts.

The archaeology of the Helmsdale valley is not only stumbled across in the haughs beside the river but also in places it blends with the fishings themselves. On the left bank of beat four, at the Baddy Wood pool is a circle of large boulders which is called locally 'the pulpit'. The river is unfordable there and the story goes that a minister would preach from this pulpit on the left bank to a congregation which gathered across the pool on the right bank. It is a nice picture. The pulpit, however, seems to me to be formed of very large and ancient stones and I wonder whether it might not belong to a much earlier, pre-Christian time, perhaps being some stones from a fortified Pictish building. That would not preclude its being used, centuries later as an impromptu pulpit. A truth about the stones, however, which I can absolutely vouch for is that they mark the best lie on the pool. I had a lovely February fish there one year, which showed in a little arc, like a taking trout, when it engulfed my fly. The lie there is formed by the pool narrowing, speeding up the flow and scouring out channels round boulders. It is, for me, the beginning of the lower and fatter part of the Helmsdale in early spring. That funnelling on the Baddy Wood pre-echoes the glorious beat three just below, the incomparable streamy and rocky pools of beat two and the wonders of the pools and streams of the lowest beat, beat one, which almost meets the tide.

There is no beat on the lower Helmsdale on which I do not have some kind of dream. Beat three is no exception. Its heart consists of two very long pools, the Upper and Lower Torrishes and I have had good spring fishing on both. Each has a fast head on a right-hand bend of the river, and each has a wide sandy tail which, with the help of a good wind, you can 'back up'. Backing up is the odd technique of starting at the bottom end of a pool like the Upper Torrish, putting a long line over the water and taking a couple of steps backwards as you fish the fly in, hand-lining too, if you want to increase the speed of the fly. It is marvellous for fresh fish, which perhaps have recently entered the pool and are lying in the easy water of the big pool before running further through the next streams and onwards. On blank days, when we have reached the late afternoon, Johnnie Sutherland, the Borrobol ghillie, the most enthusiastic, knowledgeable, helpful ghillie possible, can be relied on to look at the water and give you his advice on the best thing to do next: 'Back it up again!'

When you are aching from hard fishing and hard walking all day in a wind, these may not be the most welcome words, but I can vouch for the fact that, time and again, it has been the late afternoon backing up of one of the Torrishes which has produced the fish. I remember two from the shallowest water at the tail of the Upper Torrish one Saturday afternoon in February when we were 'toiling for a fish for the week'. I remember many others which may well have scorned a conventionally fished downstream fly, enthusiastically taking when the pool was backed up. The technique gives the fly a lovely swimming motion as it traces a wide arc over the pool towards your bank. It is a technique which needs two things – long casting, and eyes in the back of your head. I have more than once measured my length while walking backwards up a tufty or heathery bank. After all, in fishing, your eyes, your whole concentration and indeed your whole soul are out there on the pool, watching your line coming round, waiting for the pull. Feet can fend for themselves.

I happened to be fishing beat three in early March 1989 with Andrew Graham-Stewart and he reminded me that these pools were mentioned by Grey of Fallodon in his delightful book *Fly Fishing*. Andrew had a copy with him and I re-read with delight Grey's account of fishing the Torrishes exactly a hundred years previously, in early March 1889. Lord Grey refers to the Helmsdale as '*par excellence* an early spring river' and elsewhere as 'one of the best spring rivers in Scotland'. He tells us of taking two fish in 1889 in one day in early March, both from the upper part of the Lower Torrish Pool. The first, which rose four times to his fly and was rested and re-fished before it finally took, weighed 29½ pounds and the second weighed 21½ pounds, over 50 pounds in two fish! I fished that stream with great expectancy to mark the centenary of this great day, and, in the spot mentioned, I had a strong pull. But it wasn't a memorable springer. It was a large kelt. It was not the celebration of a great anniversary with a fanfare of trumpets. It was a rather *piano* event. Grey would have enjoyed the irony of that because he too suffered from dying falls in his salmon fishing, as his account goes on to relate.

On another outing, complaining of his lack of success as a salmon fisher, Grey says he only took fifteen salmon to his own rod in his March week. But, he explained, he was sharing it with a friend and only had half of the day to fish in. His complaint was not that fifteen was poor, but that the other rod, an expert by Grey's account, took over fifty fresh fish for the same six days. That was in 1891. Perhaps the most interesting part of his account of his salmon fishing, however, can be reconstructed from a footnote to his text. He says that, fishing for ten consecutive days in the best fortnight of the spring fishing on the Helmsdale, with the water in order, he not only did not take one salmon – but also he never even had a rise. He took one kelt sea trout on the last day of his stay, then, shortly after, broke his rod. The year was 1890, sandwiched between his spectacular catches of big fish in 1889 and the year of great plenty, 1891.

I cannot do other than envy Viscount Grey his fishings on the Helmsdale a century ago, but it is his blank year with the broken rod which touches my heart. I know what it feels like. In a humble way, I and my guests have enjoyed spring success too on the river. We have had some lovely fishings in late February and early March on the Helmsdale since 1976. My colleague Ian Neale had his first and second Helmsdale fish (his first two springers) on a late February day on beat one. The first was a marvellously strong ten pounder which tried to run up the far side of the island at the head of Soluscraggie on beat one. The second, whose capture I have reported in full in *Days and Nights of Game Fishing* weighed 28½ pounds and came from the Lower Caen. Grey would have liked that. My best week, for two rods, was of thirteen fish for the last week of February 1979. One beat, normally a fat one, beat six, was blank, but every other beat yielded fish, including a day of five with Rob Wilson on beat two. That day the small Gate Pool on two was boiling with fish, looking more like summer than spring. Fish were raised and missed, played and lost as well as safely landed. Yes, Grey would have liked that too. But recently, we have had three late February weeks when the yield has been two, or one or zero. It has, sometimes, become more like hunting the spring salmon than making a bag. The sensations of success are, however, heightened, in years of dearth. Any February or March Helmsdale fish is a delight. I have never seen such lovely fish, hard of body, high of shoulder, gleaming blue and pink sheens in every scale. In that strath, with all it means to those who fish it and love it, an early spring salmon on the whinny bank of beat one is a consummation longed for, a high point in the fishing year and it produces the most exquisite glow of achievement which it is hard to think of being available for anything else. Grey says:

> To me, there is nothing in all sport equal to the glory of success in salmon fishing, but the supreme moment is undoubtedly the actual hooking of the fish. However great my expectation and keenness, the feel of the fish when it hooks itself comes upon me as a shock of surprise and delight... A sense of complete achievement and satisfaction is felt merely in the hooking of it. This satisfaction in hooking a salmon remains undiminished as years go on...
> (*Fly Fishing*, p. 131).

I keep saying, that Grey would have understood some of what I and others feel for the Helmsdale as dedicated fishers for salmon. I certainly think I share the heights of his delight and the pain of his frustrations in the sport. In fact, it is difficult for those not smitten with the insuppressible urge to fish for salmon to understand what passions are involved. It is also difficult to tell people how, for me as for other fishers, the river itself is in an intimate and essential relationship with the fisher and with the whole environment. Rivers bind landscapes together; they also unite fishers of every class and persuasion, and in our fishing in them they identify fundamental human hopes and dreams. When I say the Strath of Kildonan is, for me, a spiritual place, I mean that it is a sub-lime, elemental place where I am always conscious of hopes and dreams hand in hand with very practical elements like wind and weather and fish. The Helmsdale, in its strath, for me compresses human experience and emphasises hopes and longings. It is a place where hopes rise, even at the end of a blank week. Something there lifts one up. A promise, or a half promise, keeps coming through to one from the river that, in the mysterious brown of its waters is the possibility of great solace and satisfaction. If I were writing a hymn to the Helmsdale, rather than giving this account of my fishing and my feelings there, I would insist that it ended with the Dresden amen – rising, growing, soaring and full of the promise that paradise is not illusory.

CHAPTER
2

Between the Doon and the Ayr

I WAS BROUGHT UP, sandwiched as it were, between the Doon and the Ayr. I could not have had two better tutors, although there was always a tension between them. The Ayr is a water of the Lowlands, flowing through pastures, gliding under red sandstone cliffs, easing past fruit farms and dairy pastures, splashing over its weirs to meet the sea in the middle of the town where its waters help to float fishing boats and small cargo vessels in the harbour. The Doon, which reaches the sea only two miles south of the Ayr, speaks to me of a different world. It gathers its waters in the hills well to the south of the county, drawing on moorland lochs and the weedy lanes which join them, tapping the vast reservoir of Loch Doon whose shores are backed by the highest hills in the southern uplands. From there, first rushing down the Ness Glen, then idling through a pike loch, the Doon meanders for a few miles between rushy banks as if the Waterside moorlands had foiled it. At Patna, however, the Doon discovers itself again and begins the descent of its lower valley, gathering pace through the Smithston fishings, roaring down Boreland Glen, then, reining in, it flows through attractive pools and streams, gracing estates and delighting the eye as it sweeps beside banks rich with old trees. It matures and steadies up a bit on its lower course before gliding knowingly under historic bridges and spreading over the sands at Doonfoot where it touches the waves.

Both Ayr and Doon are small rivers, thirty miles or so in each case, give or take the argument that the Doon extends many miles back through the mosses above Loch Doon where fingerling streams wind secretly through the rushes. There it is not called the Doon at all. Other identities emerge. Fishing for trout on Loch Recawr, out from Balloch-beatties Lodge, it is almost an irrelevance to bracket it with the Doon,

25

yet the older fishers there remember the occasional salmon in that loch before the raising of the levels for water supplies in the late 1930s. Salmon run still in good numbers into Loch Doon. We know this because the salmon ladder has a counter on it. When I was there recently in July, ninety fish had already run into Loch Doon. None had been caught. Loch Doon, while it may yield a chance salmon to trout fishers, is not regarded as a salmon fisher's water. I have spoken to anglers who have taken Loch Doon salmon and, typically, the stories are of trout flies being seized unexpectedly and of the salmon, if landed, being a bounty and its capture being recounted for many years as a wonder. Should there be a salmon fishery on the Loch? I doubt it. Loch Doon is a vast sheet of water. You could count a thousand fish into it and lose track of them along its rocky shoreline. I have fished the loch for its rather poor trout and have never seen a salmon moving; nor have I heard local anglers talking about their lies. If it were not for the counter on the dam, I do not think any of us would believe that more than a handful of salmon actually reach the loch. But I may be wrong. I may be speaking with prejudice, spoiled by the fact that the river from Patna to the sea offers good salmon fishing, with sea trout added, and better brown trout than the loch ever seemed to me to hold. The River Doon can be prolific. In a good year it can yield over 2000 salmon and grilse to its rods. These catches are concentrated in the twelve miles or so between Patna and Doonfoot and this represents a fishery of note which far outclasses many more renowned Highland and Hebridean waters. The river has, like many west coast waters, only the rump of a spring run. The earliest fish I have known was in March, but April and May fish are not uncommon. There are substantial summer runs of salmon, from June onwards, and in the late summer and autumn it can bring in a great variety of fish, including runs of 'grey backs', a race of larger salmon which can weigh over twenty pounds. The Doon is a small, fast river from Patna down, with many attractive, small pools and runs and only the occasional dam or dub. Throughout its length it communicates to the fisher an upland wildness which the Ayr never captures; its roots are in peaty lochs and burns and it brings an almost Hebridean feeling down to fishers at Smithston, Auchendrane, Doonholm and Alloway.

I have called the Doon my tutor for the very real reason that in my schooldays and after I learned much of the art of fishing on its waters. Sometimes the learning was bizarre. The river yielded me my first salmon from the pool in Burns Monument tea gardens, a wonderful experience, but not without its built-ironies. How could the fates have ordained that I should catch my first salmon – a wild, migratory creature, fresh from the North Atlantic – in such a manicured setting? It is ironic that what was for me an unspeakably passionate conquest took place beside immaculate terraces and paths and genteel chairs by a small bandstand. The capture was witnessed by a very pregnant lady, a Mrs Veitch from Prestwick, who had come to the hotel for quietness immediately before the birth of her twins, but who danced with excitement on the path beside me as I played the fish. The gardener gaffed it, probably his last ever fish. He had been a gamekeeper once, but then in old age kept the gardens of the hotel. Do you believe in chains of things? Beginnings and endings touching? Someone's last salmon touching someone's first? There is both a sentimental slough in the idea and a foothold of significance. I blame the Doon for blurring the difference in my own mind.

The Ayr was really my trout tutor and was well qualified to be so. The locals all called the trout there 'yellow trout' and they did and do live up to their name. There were excellent trout rising in the glides of Auchincruive, Tarholm, Enterkine, and up through Stair and Failford to the waters of Stairaird and Barskimming. It was essentially dry fly water and I have vivid memories of stalking fish under high red sandstone banks at Stairaird and finding the trout as sophisticated as any chalkstream fish might be. Indeed, when I first managed to fish a chalkstream, the Wylye near Calne, it was difficult days and evenings on the Ayr which came to my rescue and showed some of the southern trout to be not so terribly difficult after all. It was May and June fishing on the Ayr which I loved. We had good olives, bigger and darker in the early days of spring, then paler in June and better fished in the evenings. I discovered the ultimate weapon, I thought, in those trouting days, the Martins' parachute fly, whose hackles were tied horizontally, as it were, instead of round the shank of the hook. These parachutes are still used today and I cannot imagine why such flies have not become more widely known. They float well, always cock well on the surface and dry off well in false casting. I gradually narrowed down my parachute patterns for the Ayr and I ended up with two great favourites – a Greenwell size twelve which matches the olives of the earlier weeks of spring and a Light Olive Spider for the evenings in later spring and earlier summer. The Greenwell worked well as a spider too. But the secret was not just having confidence in the pattern. It also lay in making an ultra-careful approach to the rising fish. Wading had to be undertaken very gingerly and craftily. I don't know how I managed it, considering the passion of the operation with trout ahead, sucking down the flies on the deep glides. What paid off was a slow approach upstream, with long pauses to preen the fly, and blow it and see that there were no knots in the fine leader. These therapeutic pauses often helped to settle any disturbance my approach had caused and fish would come back on to the rise. I never managed to take any really large fish from the dubs of the Ayr, but I had plenty of trout from a pound to two pounds in weight. Indeed, I have only on a few occasions on other waters since seen trout of Ayr quality. The Tweed, until recently, could do as well. So could the Tay. The Don could outclass both, but size for size, the Ayr, a gentle, small pastoral river, could produce trout of high quality all demanding of the highest skill.

The Ayr produced salmon and sea trout too. When a spate came to the rivers of Ayrshire, the Ayr would rise into a very muddy flood and the Doon would also be blotted out, but the Doon would run off faster. You could be in business on the Doon a day or even two before the Ayr cleared after a spate. In this way, if you had access to both rivers, you could fish for several days on one or other water, enjoying the falling and clearing rivers which we all know are perfect for sport. Both rivers taught me a lot about coloured water for both salmon and trout. It was interesting, for instance, to see trout rising heartily to the dry fly in Ayr water which looked like milky cocoa. When you think it out, a trout poised near the surface of the stream is looking up through water whose silt content may not obliterate flies above it. From the bank, we look down into a flood and try to judge its clarity by the depths at which we can still see the shingle bed, or, when we wade, whether we can see our boots. Light has to get down through the flood and back to our eyes to give us this index of clarity. But a fish looks up from a depth selected to suit the conditions. Feeding trout in spates poise just below the surface and rise well to floating flies. Salmon also, in all but the most turgid waters can often see a fly or bait above them, and take it.

The Ayr is a river which characteristically clouds with sandy soil and produces a light-coloured brown spate. The Doon also rises to carry silt, but it is soil from a darker land. Doon floods carry peaty waters too. The Ayr takes longer than the Doon to clear after a spate, but the Doon may lose fishing because of dark, peaty water at the tail end of a flood which seems to sicken salmon and sea trout. I have often been defeated on the banks of the Doon in perfect water height when peaty water made the fishing dour. You might imagine that after many years of trying, I would have evolved a technique to deal with this, but the fact is that I am still baffled by it on the Doon and elsewhere. It is not just the dark colour. I have caught salmon on Highland and Lowland rivers in brown water. For example, waters like the Helmsdale in Sutherland, which never loses its peaty colour, fishes well despite the dark brown tinge. This troublesome black water is acid, often has a lot of fibre in it and it can leave the sand on the bottom of the river stained. Water of this sort has been standing stale in high moorland pools and ditches, some within soft woodlands, some on the hill. A good flood will bring it down with a rush to the valley below. It is dourness in liquid form. I am one of many Doon anglers who blame upland forestry management for these acid, damaging spates and I have no doubt that the problem grew as the hills above were planted using the techniques of the 1950s. Many of the hills around Recawr and Mackaterick, high in the Doon system, which were grass and rushes and open peat when I walked and fished there as a boy, are now set among dense conifer forests. These forests were planted on open hill land where the ploughing was the first serious disturbance of the moors since the ice ages. In this method of planting, the plough turns over great ridges of hill, often across the contours, and the trees are planted on top of the upturned ridges. The ploughing leaves deep furrows which trap water and in floods, this stale, acid water from the forestry flashes into the hill burns, producing surges of sour water which stain the river below and make fishing dour. Recent improvements in hill forestry management have brought about a return to planting directly into the peat without ploughing. Further, new standards of forest layout have resulted in trees being kept well back from hill burns or other watercourses, thus allowing rainwater running off the hill to be filtered by the soil and to leach out many of the dangerous chemicals present in this drainage. But even with these improvements, afforested hill still drains too quickly and too directly into the river system, and still brings down water of high acidity which in the aftermath of floods makes fishing dour, and more seriously in the long term, reduces the fertility of the river with all the implications that has for the growth of salmon and trout fry.

Fishing the Doon for salmon in my salad days brought me into contact with a tradition of salmon fishing which, I was later to realise, was a hangover from old styles and attitudes and which my generation of fly fishers was to question and replace. In the 1950s and 1960s, if you looked into a salmon fisher's fly box on the Doon or Ayr, you would see two distinct types of fly. There were, first of all, garish flies, all tinsel and golden pheasant, flies which you would have seen in most Edwardian fly books. Among them you would see the Silver Doctor, the Silver Wilkinson, the Durham Ranger, the Jock Scott and the Dusty Miller, all tied on single hooks. They looked magnificent; indeed, it was quite normal to make them into brooches for presents. They caught fish, especially in floods, and looking back, they were fished almost as a bait might be, well sunk, swept round, worked by the rod and handlined in. But in Ayrshire there were also much dowdier flies, tied locally, usually with unmixed wings of turkey and dubbed wool bodies. These dull turkey, bittern and mallard wing flies were, I was later to discover, very similar in type to the local flies on Tweedside described by Scrope in *Days and Nights of Salmon Fishing*. You will remember them – *Toppy* (with its wing taken from a white-tipped turkey tail feather), *Meg wi' the Muckle Mou'* (tied from a brown turkey tail) and *Meg in her Braws* (with wings, light brown from the wing of a bittern). I had a set of these nineteenth century Tweed flies tied up recently, snelled directly to gut – to bring them, as it were, from the Haghe etchings in Scrope's book directly into my hand – and the appearance of them immediately brought together the older Tweed tradition and that of the Doon as if all these old flies shared the same philosophy. Scrope first listed them on Tweed in 1843; I fished similar flies in 1950 on the Doon and the Ayr.

I well remember the Grey Turkey and the Brown Turkey which looked like outsize trout wet flies, dun in colour, with wings of single feathers or strips, not mixed fibres. I accepted these old flies on the Doon as one might accept porridge – local, full of goodness but possibly lacking in subtlety. I caught salmon on them and I liked the way the sober colours blended with the bracken and the moor, but I became less and less happy with them in their heavy, single-hooked form. Even as a young angler, I did not like the stiffness of the turkey wings, nor the sail-and-keel attitude these flies adopted in the water. I was suspicious of the hooking powers of the heavy single hooks they were normally tied on and I did not like the overdressing which characterised them. I liked them best in small sizes such as eights and when I discovered the Loch Lomond turkey-winged flies in the mid-1950, much more lightly dressed, slender flies, I brought them down to the Doon and began to take salmon and sea trout on them.

The real revolution on Doon and Tweed was to come from a different source, however – from the Aberdeenshire Dee. In the late 1950s I saw for the first time a series of small, hairwing tubes, Sharpe's Parker tubes, I was struck by two things. Firstly, how small they were, mere wisps of stoat's tail or bucktail, tied on small plastic tubes half an inch to one inch in length. Secondly, I was greatly attracted to their sober colours. There was a tiny Hairy Mary tied with squirrel, a Stoat's Tail and others, all with dull little bodies. They were fished with small trebles, down to size fourteen which gave the lie to the local wisdom, that a large single iron was needed to hook and hold a salmon. It was a real change of direction. For me, and for many salmon fishers, it was also a revolution, away from single hooks and gaudy colours on the one hand and from stiff singles on the other, although, interestingly, the colours of the local flies were in sympathy with the new little tubes.

I was fishing Nether Auchendrane on the Doon one July in a falling water, just after getting my first half dozen of these small tubes, Stoat's tail, Hairy Mary and Lady Caroline. Grilse were running and I took three fish when others, fishing single hooked flies, were complaining that the grilse were coming unstuck because of soft mouths. It was a day of enlightenment. I do not think I fished a single-hooked turkey ever again. The small tubes changed not only my fly box but also my whole attitude to salmon fly fishing. I used to fish them on my trout rod and take salmon from all manner of small pots and runs which might not look like salmon lies to people used to larger rivers. Sometimes in summer I would move a salmon to a trout fly and quickly switch my cast to one carrying a small tube and I would often take the fish. On Smithston, fishing for trout, I saw a splash in a small run called the Scoot Hole and, tying on a half-inch Stoat's Tail I took the fish in low water conditions in August, typical of the new fly fishing for the new age.

By an excellent stroke of luck, neary forty years after my apprenticeship on the Doon, I have forged a new connection with the river. I am on the management committee of the newly formed Smithston Fishings, which have brought under one management three beats I fished as a young angler – Smithston, Carnochan and Polnessan. This lovely varied fishery, with moorland holding pools at the top, including the famous Thorn Tree Pool near Polnessan from which the record Doon grey back was taken, 36½ pounds, has a long series of lovely rocky runs and lies in its middle section, which become more and more brisk as the river turns into the narrow valley below and plunges to Boreland Glen at the end of our water. We have begun to add art to nature on that streamy water. We have started to produce a whole series of new pools in what was often shallow trout water, doing this sympathetically, using the stones from the river bed to blend with the bank, creating new channels and lies and giving the streamy section a whole new dimension in salmon fishing. In our first season we had the delight of seeing many of our new pools producing fish to fly. In the past, many of the salmon in the faster glen lies were caught on the worm. While this is often the only way you can fish certain lies in certain heights of water, there was far too much dunking of worms done in the past. Now that we have new pools, a whole new field of fly fishing has opened up. Worm can be used skilfully in many places still, but my preferences are for the fly.

Comparing how we fish on the Doon now with the techniques and tackle of my apprenticeship days, I am conscious that yet another big change has taken place, even since the coming of the small tubes. We now prefer our flies produced as dressed trebles – Drury style flies, tied on tens and eights mostly, on sharp little Partridge hooks – Shrimps, Stoat's Tails, Willie Gunns and Hairy Marys. These little flies are fished often on single-handed rods, mostly on the floater, having enough weight in their hooks to avoid skating on the surface even in the fast glides. So I find myself each summer and autumn, back on the river of my boyhood, many years and many salmon later, remembering the lies where I last hooked fish, and covering them with small dressed trebles, occasionally doubles, or in higher water tubes. It is a marvellous renewal of an old friendship in which much has changed, but much remains unaltered.

Tackle has changed and has changed our fishing. We now have, for smaller salmon rivers, excellent single handed carbon rods, eleven feet or so long, ideal for tireless fishing over small lies, stroking the fly over the glassy water between streams, dangling it down a run, casting accurately to a pothole behind a stone. Salmon fishing has distanced itself in time and in materials from the heavy greenheart rod of my boyhood, and from the longer built-cane rods which I now find that, fit as I am, I have hardly the bottle to fish all day. Double-handed carbon rods are, of course, also delightful and give casting and mending power for the larger pools. But I do not think that salmon hooked on the smaller rods are any more difficult than those on the longer ones. At best you might be two or three minutes longer in the fight, but in return, you might find that the more intimate contact with the fish is more than enough compensation. When I was in Alaska in 1989, fishing very much larger waters than any I cover in Scotland, I fished my eleven foot Bruce and Walker Century heavy duty and found no real difficulty with silver salmon and sockeye. Indeed, I have, in the years since, wondered why I go on all the time with my fifteen-foot carbon rod in Scotland. The answer lies in the way the long rod spey casts, the way it throws out waddingtons and larger tubes in heavy water, the way it rolls out lines and forms the most castable of loops. But in this, I am not thinking about the Doon. There, an angler could fish a single-handed rod at all times of the year and would find it no disadvantage, rather a source of added pleasure.

The Doon too has changed. It is, as a whole river, better managed and cared for than it ever was. The Improvement Association and the much more active District Board form a basis of management in which individual fisheries can thrive. The imminent possiblity of buying off the nets in the estuary raises interesting hopes for the future. There is better bailiffing, and less serious poaching. All this has, however, not in any way changed the character and atmosphere of the river. It is still a river which graces the Lowlands with hill water; it is still a marvellous, productive little salmon river with a good crop of sea trout and browns. I have not returned to find it wasted; I have come back to find it in excellent form, on the up-and-up, just as wild, just as talkative, just as challenging as it ever was. Indeed, the river seems to know something about its own future. It flows now as if, with nets off and good management, it will excel itself. I do not think that this is an excessive claim.

CHAPTER
3

The island of Mull

Sᴇᴀ ᴄʀᴏssɪɴɢs to the island of Mull are often extraordinary journeys of translation; you quite unambiguously commit yourself not only to a new and separate place but also to a different frame of mind. When you leave Oban and the shelter of its bay, the Firth of Lorne can bring you Atlantic winds which set the ferry rolling. Then, as you pass Lismore, where tides froth round the rocks beside the lighthouse, you are aware of going through a kind of gate into the Sound of Mull. Duart Castle watches from its rocky headland to the west as you sail in towards Craignure. Look then for many changes of colour. The sea will be deep blue over kelp and a stunning emerald over sand. Behind, the slopes of Mull will define themselves in many shades of green – grass by the shoreline, forests patched behind, and darkening, the rushy and grassy hills rise massively, sometimes into the cloud. At that point you can begin to think of Scotland differently. You have left it behind. You have crossed the main and you would not be very different from a host of others if you felt as you did so that you were changed. Mull lifts before you, like a new land, atmospheric, sometimes secretive, very enticing, and full of fishing promise.

As a young fisher, I learned to read Mull first from the Atlantic side, where the island is penetrated by long sea lochs with wonderful sands, golden above the tide and luminous green beneath. I went there first as a boy with a bicycle, looking for loch fishing for trout. Then I returned to work as a student on Iona helping to set up the Abbey and take part in its youth programmes. One summer I led a group of boys on a project on Mull near Bunessan, where we helped to run a small, remote, salmon netting station at Camas. On all of these visits I fished in the lochs and rivers of Mull, or tried to tempt the many sea trout which fed among the seaweed all along the shoreline, usually unsuccessfully.

When I did hook a fish off these shores on the fly, it was nearly always, alas, a small saithe.

The Ross of Mull was where my early fishing developed – that ancient pre-Cambrian arm with rocks like boilerplating which runs west to Fionnphort, and looks across the narrow sound to Iona. Appropriately enough the nearest loch to Iona was called Poit na h-I (pronounced *Potee*), the Stewpond of Iona. It was a small loch lying on a stony moor and draining south to the white sands of Fidden. I used to fish there in the late evening and it was a generous place, full of quarter- and half-pound brown trout but not in any way fitting the stereotype of the stewpond – not at all like the Franklin's lush stewpond in Chaucer's Prologue which reflected his stables full of the finest horses, his larder filled with the best ale and delicacies, his coops filled with fat partridges and his stewpond: 'And many a bream and many a luce in stew...'.

Poit na h-I had its own wealth – lingering sunsets of the richest reds and oranges and sights to the north west of the dark blue outlines of the Treshnish Isles. The water was often burnished by the colour of the sky and in this ethereal surface, trout rose. Sometimes there I took trout in the most dramatic setting, to the sound of the distant tolling of the Abbey bell floating to me over the Sound of Iona. It was trout fishing at its most atmospheric and it produced in me feelings of absolute peace.

I often wondered if Poit na h-I held sea trout. The sandy bays and weedy coves near Fidden were alive with them, uncatchably veeing in and out of the seaweed. I wondered if the burn between the loch and the sea could ever flood enough to bring the fish up. Each evening I fished, I looked for signs of sea trout, but saw none until one late dusk I was casting over a small bay when I saw the most enormous rise in the low light. Then, a few seconds later I saw another, closer, almost within casting distance. Were these the first sea trout? I was lengthening line to cover the area when there was a boil on the water near me and I was startled. Up through the surface came a head, then not far behind up came another. Otters! They looked at me, stretching their necks out of the loch, then in a fast arched dive, both were away. They had looked at me, a miserable, inefficient fisher, and had fled. *They* knew whether there were sea trout in the loch. They knew, because they owned it. I reeled in. The bay was calm now, but without rises, and the light had dwindled to a soft dimness. I left the stewpond to its rightful owners and, rubbing off as many midges as I could, I walked back over the moor to the Fionnphort road.

I fished many waters on Mull in these early days, on a kind of exploratory basis, wondering what might be in them. I was told in Bunessan that Loch Assapol, nearby, held only a few finnock and no salmon because the burn was choked. When I asked why the burn was not cleared out to let the fish through, no one seemed to have a good answer. I fished Assapol anyway and saw nothing better on that first trip than a few half-pound finnock. A number of years later, returning to Bunessan with my family, I fished Assapol again, expecting much the same. For the first hour it was a repetition of the old days, bringing nothing to the fly worth taking. My two sons, then seven and five, were beginning to get cold and the elder wondered when we would go home. Then, out of the corner of my eye, near a stone dyke we were drifting past, I saw a salmon move. We were already almost past it, so I leapt to the oars and pulled the boat off a little way and set it on the right drift. I had a fairly light sea trout cast on, but that would do. First cast over the water where the rise had been he came, taking a Dark Mackerel on the dropper. He took off into the loch and happily the wind helped us to follow. What a lively fish, running, circling the boat, sounding and surfacing! Mark my younger son was excited, pleading with me not to lose the fish. Nicholas was not much moved. He thought it was all taking a long time and he wondered when we might get back to shore as he was feeling cold and would like to have his tea! I had, with luck, a small telescopic gaff in the bottom of my fishing bag and using this (the last fish I have ever used a gaff on), I managed to bring the fish aboard. It was over nine pounds. When we got ashore, the farmer who had given me the boat came down and looked at the fish lying on the shingle and sent for his family to come and look. It was the first salmon off Assapol for years and the biggest he had seen. He wanted his children to see it. I wonder if they have seen another in the many years since that happened? They will have, if someone has taken the trouble to clean out the burn.

Mull in those days in the 1950s and 1960s had a relaxed feeling to all its life. Hayfields gently returned to rushes; houses quietly slid into disrepair. Things have changed on the island in many ways now. Visitors have turned into tourists. In some ways things have gingered up but, over four decades, I have never lost the sense that there is, on Mull, a notable lack of urgency in getting things done. I have often thought that it might be a virtue, valuing time on a span unknown on the mainland. Perhaps, if I lived on Mull long enough, I would grasp the principles of such a life. I feel that, however, if I lived in Bunessan, I would still struggle against the non-urgency of some of the life there. Yet, I would not want the island to be too developed. I would not want it to lose its peaceful qualities. It is a paradox. We desire the islands for many reasons, but mainly because we need their unspoiled peace, yet many of our instincts are to tamper with that peace, even to ravish it. The unanswered question in my mind is whether it is better to have the chance of one salmon of high memorability in an untroubled place, or to organise and have several, but in the process of improving, lose the

cherished ambience of the place. Assapol has at least solved the
problems of restraint; encounters with good sea trout and salmon are
rare. No angler fishes greedily there. Any success is cherished.

Mull has a wasp waist from Salen to Loch na Keal, where no more
than three miles separate its east from its west coast. Yet, thirty miles
of road run west between Craignure and Iona Ferry. As if in a kind of
balance above and below the waist, two substantial lochs lie, one north,
Loch Frisa and one south, Loch Ba. Both lochs lie in the famous north-
west/south-east attitude and and both are drained by salmon rivers. It
would be quite reasonable to look for similarity of fishing, but you
would seek in vain. Frisa is a generous trout loch with the occasional
finnock and sea trout and a rare salmon; Ba is a salmon and sea trout
loch with the very occasional good brown trout. There is a social divide
too. Ba is fished from the lodges of two large island estates, with some
special access through them to visitors. Frisa is fished mostly by day
permits obtained from the Forestry Commission. Ba is in excellent
stalking territory with good hills to the west and the east, where,
fishing in October, the air is full of the roaring of rutting stags. Frisa
lies more than five miles long between forests and moor, speaking a
different language from Ba. You can feel this clearly in the boat when
you are drifting each loch. On Frisa, the boat will most likely be
drifting down the shallow rocky western shore where birch and rowan
hang over the water and ten trout might be risen in as many minutes.
Talk in the Frisa boat is wide ranging. Fishers sit relaxed, casting wet
flies, talking, laughing. On Ba the boats, the rods and the drifts and the
talk are altogether different. Those who are dapping for sea trout, hold
their long rods up with a great seriousness and significance and watch
the dapping fly mesmerically. Ba has long drifts, not always productive, which only makes the concentration more intense. The fly rolls
and skips and tips on the water and every moment is coloured by a
tense expectation that there will be a swirl, a sudden leap, a large head
with an open mouth and perhaps the fly will go down and a sea trout
might be hooked. Ba is bigger time than Frisa but Frisa has a picnic
feeling to it and many fish to cheer you up, a family place, a loch of
many touches, takes, tugs splashes. It is a loch of wild brown half
pounders and better, and if a finnock comes to the fly, or a rare sea
trout, it is a minor wonder.

In my early days on Mull, my Poit na h-I and Frisa days, I had no
access to Ba, except one evening when I plucked up courage and
knocked at the door of Gruline House and the tenant said, yes, I could
fish Ba from the shore. I made my way to the banks, set up my trout
flies and waded along casting here and there, expecting trout or
finnock. Instead I had an almighty heave, the sensation of being into a
great fish and the sudden collapse of contact as my trout cast broke.

That fish had to be a salmon. When I think of that incident now, having fished Ba many times since trying for salmon with the right tackle, although I have moved salmon many times, I have, for some reason never had one off the loch. This may be because most of my fishing there has been in autumn, and the bulk of salmon are then stale. Ba usually yields its salmon to the fly in the drifts up near the head of the loch, or round the shore near Benmore Lodge. As on many large lochs, many of the salmon are taken by trolling. Boats troll out to the fly drifts at the head, fly fish all day and troll back in the late afternoon. I have never found Ba salmon, river or loch, easy fish to tempt, which makes it all the more remarkable that in my boyhood, on that first evening I contacted one on a trout fly on waters well away from the usual drifts. What force directs a beginner's fly like that, covering a salmon and tempting it with a trout fly on an unknown water in what I realise now was an unlikely place? Don't just say it was luck. That's not an explanation; rather an excuse for the lack of one. This chance cast and chance success is in the make up of Mull. I chanced, as a boy, to cast my fly on the Forsa and took a four-and-a-half pound sea trout, my first ever. There is a kind of smiling of the gods at work when this sort of thing happens. Sometimes it leads to a memorable loss; sometimes to a catch which comes ashore despite fumbling and ineptitude and inadequate tackle.

Ba is a curious and compelling place and its short river is a place of wonder. Thirty years after losing my chance salmon on the loch, through a great friend of mine who settled on Mull and ran an excellent fishing lodge there, I had the chance to get to know the river and the loch quite well. I usually fished both river and loch late in the season in September and October, but I have tried both in June and July too. On the river, one longed for a flood. In Mull a flood comes and goes suddenly. Pools change shape and character. In a falling flood you can fish a large pool on a corner in the morning with its streams and eddies and draw off, and in the afternoon when you try it again, it has altered so much that you hardly recognise the pool as the same place. In the river Ba in a falling spate, you cannot fish the same pool twice. Each time down is different. This makes fishing a small river like the Ba show an infinite variety with constantly changing conditions, not the least of which is when the salmon and sea trout run, where they stop, how they should be covered with the fly and what they will do when they are hooked.

I remember fishing down a pool on a bend, adopting the conventional approach of covering the stream and letting the fly sweep round in to my bank. I touched nothing. Walking back up the river in an hour's time I saw the pool from a new angle and I saw it differently. I saw that the stream was not where the salmon might be and the great eddy which the pool formed out in the middle between two runs was the focus of the place. But how was it to be fished? I decided on a strategy. I put on a small brass tube fly and, casting upstream, I fished the eddy, holding the line up to allow the brass tube to get down fairly quickly and fish the few yards of gentle, turning water where the holding place was. I was, in one sense, fishing the pool backwards to cover the reverse stream of the eddy. I had a take and hooked a nine-and-a-half-pound salmon, the best I have ever had off the Ba.

On another occasion, fishing every pool down from Knock and getting nothing, I eventually arrived at two long pools where the river changed direction and flowed at right-angles among rushy banks before making a second ninety degree turn and heading for the sea pool. I got nothing in the top pool until, feeling slightly despondent, I threw the fly more or less directly across the stream and letting the flow pull it round quickly, had a strong take, probably from a good sea trout, as the fly sped across. I moved down to the second pool and fished it through normally. Nothing. Then I decided to speed up the last cast by throwing a long line over to the far bank, and walking backwards as if backing up. The fly raced across and I again had a strong pull. I repeated the cast and had no further luck. What I did then was probably just a little bit careless. Not paying very much attention and with the line still on the pool, I turned and walked away up the bank with my rod stuck out at right angles across the water, a slovenly and ill-controlled action. I began reeling in as I went. I had suddenly a great pull which unfortunately my rod absorbed much of, followed by a great splashing and pulling as a salmon or a sea trout of salmon size thrashed on top of the water. I hate to see thrashing; it almost always means nose hooking. I quickly got on to terms with the fish, as I thought, but a run or two later the hooks fell out. Every time I have returned to these pools, I have spent my time trying to make the fast fly work again and I think I managed in several years of trying, to get one more pull. But I have never landed a fish from that auspicious place. It is fascinating that at a certain height that pool would fish only with a ridiculously fast swinging fly when normal covering of the water produced nothing. At most heights, that pool was dead.

These 'walking away' takes are interesting. I have taken fish on the Naver, the Helmsdale, the Doon and the Dee doing this. Indeed, as a matter of practice when I have waded down a pool, say on the Dee, I always walk out with the last long cast on the water, swinging round often quite quickly, below me. I have seen others doing this, putting the rod over their shoulder. I tend to carry the rod at its point of balance, but always keeping the tip pointing towards the fly and leaving the reel free to turn with the take. I have had some splendid takes in this way from fish which had refused my fly fished normally down over them.

Mull taught me part of this trick, even if Mull, in typical character, was not very consistent in bringing offers to the walking-out technique.

Above the road bridge of the Ba the river has only about half a mile to go to the point at which it leaves the loch, gathering its waters into a series of small pools and glides, one of which is known as 'The Flats'. This is a splendid place to fish, and it will give you great sport if you are subtle about it. This is a place, *par excellence*, for the dropper. We fished size eight Invictas there on single-handed trout or sea trout rods and we treated the salmon as if they were sea trout. We crept to the bank, stood well back or, more normally, knelt, or crawled to the river and fished the fly so that the dropper vee-ed the surface over the stream right under our own bank. The salmon rises there were just like trout. There would be a little rise, an arc with a hint of colour in the stream, and the fish would be on. Thereafter all resemblance to trout fishing ceased with the fish tearing around on the trout rod and causing all manner of anxieties. A small, red salmon took me there one October and ran vigorously down through two pools before I managed to net it out, almost at the road bridge. That little fish was *so* powerful and gave unmatched sport on the single-handed rod.

It was at the flats also, one September evening, when I was trying to blend with the bank and dibble my dropper over the near stream, that a stag with a head as big as a tree appeared on the other side of the Ba, scented the air, then marched into the river with high strides, and like a romantic painting, stood in the middle majestically, looking down to where I knelt on the bank. The stag was frozen in a regal pose in the middle of that Hebridean stream, backed by birches, pines, heather and the tall hill. I don't know whether he saw me or scented me, but he suddenly turned almost in disdain, crossed to my bank fifty yards above, and trotted off towards the loch. Those who know the Highlands only from chocolate box tops and advertisements for oatcakes may think that stags are always there, standing royal and dignified with the blue hills behind. Let them think, then, that my moment with the stag on the Ba was nothing special. I know, however, that the encounter was amazing, a rare and beautiful experience, an unforgettable moment of harmony and balance. The rod and the river, the birches and the hill, the angler and the stag were, for a moment, all one, a perfect suspended experience, removed in all its aspects by the greatest gulf from the cliché of the biscuit box and the illustrated calendar.

Loch Ba has drifts over bays, past points, along wooded shorelines and, right at the head, a series of drifts over a shallowing estuary where the top river enters. There you will see salmon crashing out of the water along the steep shingle shore to the south-west. You will see sea trout leaping high out of the loch. If the wind is favourable, you can

drift in from one shore from the west and with luck manage a drift out
of the estuary along to the south-eastern shore to the burn among the
trees where the Knock beat ends. I have had some lovely sea trout on
the wet fly on these drifts and have lost better, but I have not taken a
salmon, although I have raised several. My fishings may be rather late
for loch salmon. They are best taken shortly after their arrival from the
sea. Loch fish in late summer and autumn are usually fickle and are
often stale and they tantalise you with their boiling rises which lead to
nothing but raised hopes. It was on that drift that I saw a sea eagle.
These rare birds were re-introduced to Scotland and established themselves on the island of Rhum. A pair came to Mull in the mid 1980s and
frequented Loch Ba. We were drifting down the eastern shore at the
head when we saw the great bird flying up the loch and 200 yards ahead
of our drifting boat, turning into a clump of small trees. When we
reached the end of our drift we had only to nudge the boat fifty yards
forward to ease round the point to the small bay in which the eagle had
settled. It rose suddenly from a pine tree and with great wings spread,
eight feet from tip to tip, it came towards us in a great glide, as if
looking for currents of air to lift it. The sea eagle passed directly over
our heads, not thirty feet up, before rising with the wind and crossing
to land on the other side of the loch. On the tree which it had left was
a massive nest, a cacophany of branches, sticks and heather, locked into
the heart of the pine, ludicrously like a double bed which some up-
heaval had placed there and mammocked.

I fished lochs and rivers all over Mull in the course of nearly four
decades, discovering two pound brown trout in the Mishnish lochs,
good sea trout in the Glen More lochs and the Lussa below, salmon and
sea trout in the Aros and elsewhere.

In the right mood, Mull offers all the variety of Hebridean game
fishing that you might dream of. But in one recent summer, Mull
revealed to me something unpredicted, something remarkable,
probably unique in Scotland – salmon rod fishing in the sea. Let me be
slightly vague about where this happened. In the north of Mull a sea
loch with rocky banks has a narrow section no broader than a large
river and through this the sea floods to fill a large sandy inner loch into
which a little river flows. When the tide floods, a salt sea river is formed
flowing inland. When the tide ebbs a reverse river is formed, flowing
seawards. At certain times of the year salmon appear in the sea loch in
considerable numbers and as the tides transform the narrows into a
river, they cavort and splash and rove and show there as they might in
a series of streams and pools in a Highland river.

One summer, in hot weather, when the rest of Mull was in drought,
my friend who lived nearby decided to fish there in the sea for salmon.
You might well think, as I thought, that this would be a waste of time.

Salmon really do not take lures in salt water, do they? Well, they do, but the only place I have ever seen it has been in that salt water flow and it was fascinating. They would not take fly, although I thought that a deeply sunk large tube might do it. They did take spoons, and plugs, including a Kynoch Killer, that ice-cream cone of a plug usually fished behind boats on the river Tay. We used to watch salmon there, apparently foraging in small shoals among the sea weed and revelling in the stream caused by the tides. My Mull friend thought much about this remarkable place and its unique fishing for salmon and studied it in different conditions. He tried all manner of approaches and lures and, in due course, almost as a joke, he tried a bunch of worms. A bunch of worms in the sea! Absolute madness! It was, however, inspired madness. It was amazingly successful, once you had mastered the technique of presenting a waving bunch of worms among the dense columns of seaweed in the salt stream. The water was clear and you could sometimes see the whole process. Grilse and salmon would apparently forage up into the stream as if searching for food, often looking as if they were hunting in packs. This was an extraordinary sight. Didn't we all know that salmon which have arrived inshore to run the rivers do not feed? The digestive tracts have atrophied as part of the process of returning to fresh water. Ergo, the fish were obviously not feeding. Well, you could have fooled me. These fish looked as if they were actively foraging and actively feeding, even if they were not. They came to the worm as if they scented it and wanted to feed on it. They took the worm as if they wanted to eat it, and they took it well. Of course salmon in fresh water follow baits and take bunches of worms, and prawns and shrimps. Unsuspecting coarse fishers have hooked salmon on maggots. Perhaps if we saw our river fish as clearly as we were able to see the salmon in that sea river on Mull, we would accept that all salmon takes demonstrate the urge to feed, even if their ability to do anything with the food has gone. These Mull salt-water fish, however, looked heartier about feeding than any I have seen actually taking in fresh water. During that summer the salt-water river yielded a good number of fish. Many were grilse, but some were salmon of the eight- to ten-pound class. Interestingly, some of the salmon were quite coloured. All the fish I saw taken had sea lice on them. The implications of this are that some perfectly fresh salmon are coloured when they leave the sea and enter the river. Alternatively, some salmon migrate back to sea after colouring in the river. We know little about this. Other interesting issues emerged. It seemed to those of us fishing this sea beat that the numbers of fish in that rush of water were far above the stock likely to run the nearby small river. Even if you assumed that they were heading for other Mull rivers, many of which were miles away, they still represented a large stock. Were these salmon, cavorting in our sea river, fish which would go much further and run rivers on the mainland nearby – the Shiel, the Lochy, the Awe? I do not know. They were not local fish anyway. The local river could not have held them. The questions remain unanswered. I have a very strong sense that we experienced an exceptional place in an exceptional summer. Did we go back? Yes, and some fish were seen and caught in subsequent years, but never in the quantities nor with the *elan* they displayed when my friend Ian discovered them in that first year.

The uniqueness of that place in Mull is obviously connected to the shape of the sea loch and the remarkable running tide race. I could not look at it without my mind going back to the Evripos in Greece, the baffling sea river which flows under the 'black bridge' at Khalkis on the the island of Evvoia. The Aegean tides, like the whole Mediterranean system, are not high, perhaps measuring fifteen inches a day, nothing like Mull where a spring tide can give you fifteen feet or more. Yet the Evripos flows and forms a sea river of the oddest sort. You would expect two flows and two ebbs a day, but this extraordinary set of narrows has anything between six and fourteen changes of flow a day. The ancient philosophers all, in their turn, tried to explain it. Was it caused by back tides round the large island of Evvoia? To this day the phenomenon has never been satisfactorily explained. There is a story that Aristotle studied the Evripos sea river and failing to solve its flows, threw himself in to the water in despair! I spent several months in Khalkis right beside the Evripos, when I was learning Greek, and I watched the tide-river flowing, stopping, changing, flowing backwards, endlessly. Using a snorkel, I also watched the way the mullet, garfish and bass used to respond to the currents, taking up their positions in the stream as trout might in a run. I wonder what Aristotle would have made of our Mull river. He would have found the tides easier to explain, for a start. But how would he have explained the salmon taking in the sea, and doing it so enthusiastically that particular summer? And assuming Aristotle knew what a good fishing week was, would he not have marvelled that, for a few weeks, that ebb and flow sea river fished better than many a beat on a great river on the mainland?

I have a hunch that the success we had in the sea that year was directly related to the drought. I have for some time now been very interested in the phenomenon of downstream migration of salmon. We assume that a salmon which runs up into freshwater stays up and seldom or never drops back. I know of several waters where salmon run up stony rivers in spates and as the waters fall, drop back to the lower pools and the sea. In low water, is it not reasonable to believe that salmon would drop back to the coastal waters from the diminished Mull and Ardnamurchan rivers and join new fish also waiting for water to run?

The Mull sea river set me thinking about where similar fishing conditions might exist in Scotland but while there are many good tidal races in the islands I have yet to hear of any which has been successfully fished for salmon in the sea. So part of the mystery remains – all the more so because the Mull river was distinctly unrewarding in subsequent summers.

I think I am happy to leave Mull to keep the secret of that salt water phenomenon. It seems in keeping with an island which has, over several decades, regularly produced surprises for me. Mull has so often brought out the unusual, often with a chuckle in it, that I sometimes wonder if it isn't all intentional – the otters pretending they were sea trout, the sea eagle and its double bed, the fly cast to a big foraging sea trout among the seaweed, only to produce a small saithe. Mull's sense of the ridiculous and the extraordinary are blended. There is a bizarre bounty there, like my first sea trout being my largest for years, and frustration too, like my spending hours and hours trying for these massive sea trout vee-ing in and out of the bladder wrack, and giving my flies tantalising follows and swirls, but never a take. There is a nod and a wink perceptible in Mull experiences, if you have the gift to detect them. That green island is telling you that you are not on the mainland any more, that different rules apply. George Macleod of Iona used to say that only a tissue separated time from eternity on Iona. I have felt that there, but the more I wander and fish on Mull, Iona's mother and father, the more I have felt something uncanny, if less metaphysical – that Mull was conscious of us as we fished. Mull becomes close, personal, generous, playful and sulky. I think Mull anglers with an eye to see and an ear to hear learn this. Many fishers feel as I do that the sight of the hills of Mull from Morvern stirs great longings to return and fish. Mull 'winds us in'. But as I feel this longing, I confess I also feel a twinge of fear. I am afraid that, one year, I shall return to Mull and will find it changed for the worse – too developed, too touristy – and my fear is that we will lose our personal contact with this excellent island in this way. I could not bear to return to Mull, which nourished me as a young fisher, and find that it was now all rationalised, spoken for – that all its secret places were known. What a loss it would be to return and find its palaces full of false suitors.

CHAPTER
4

Sweet darkness

I HAVE OFTEN FISHED for sea trout right through the night in rivers such as the Spey or the Border Esk or the Dee but the sweetest nights I can remember have been in the West Highlands. Fishing there, on the Shiel for example, one usually finds oneself wishing that the nights were longer and the darkness deeper. In late June, which is the best of the season in my view, there seems to be barely three hours of darkness, with long, lingering gloamings as the light fades, and, in the lightest nights, dusk blends with dawn. These are the white nights of the West Highlands and in such conditions, sea trout can be almost as wary as they are by day. Summer nights, when they are on form, can be something of a sandwich. If you were to try a sea trout fly delicately down a stream as the light goes you might very well find yourself playing a salmon. If you linger on the pools after dawn, you might again find salmon taking. In between, it is sea trout time, but from time to time a salmon may seize your flies and force you to play it precariously in the dark. A salmon at dusk on a sea trout evening is bad news, spoiling the quietness of the sea trout streams and pools and wasting time. Most devoted sea trout fishers would rather hold their hand than risk hooking a salmon in their prime sea trout glide. But a salmon at dawn is marvellous news. It is a way to end your night's fishing with a trumpet blast.

Darkness increases your chances of taking sea trout, but most certainly does not guarantee it. Nights are not uniform. They begin, establish themselves and end, and their patterns will usually dictate how you fish. After many years of night fishing I have come to expect the night to be fairly well marked out into phases, and most nights oblige. The light fades, draining the colours from the grass and trees and we expect the evening rise; the night settles and the fish are in their first

44

phase of the night proper. Then comes the lull, the changeover time, as if the night is no longer the property of the day before, but is programming itself to be the darkness before the new dawn. This second phase of darkness is usually the problematic one. Sea trout seem to go down and, as if in harmony, all around on the bank is at its quietest and darkest. This is the phase when we try sunk fly as opposed to a fly near the surface for the night sea trout, but the formula does not always work as neatly as that. Nor does the formula for the dawn rise work every time. Dawn can break cold. Even in summer a heavy dew, almost a frost, can make you shudder. The river can steam with cold mist or a wind can stir at dawn and chill the surface of the pools. These are the mornings which often foretell a change in the weather and sea trout dislike them.

On the upper Spey, where I have often fished in June and early July for sea trout on a marvellous, deep sandy pool called Kinhurdy, I have seen every rule about phases of the night broken. Interestingly, I can hardly remember the nights when everything went well, but I have an indelible memory of nights when the opposite was true. Let me illustrate. One June evening I found the river at a perfect height. Fish were showing in the deep backwaters of the pool. The water was low but not stale. It was mild and windless. I sat almost fretting on the bank waiting for the light to go to allow me to try the glides at the tail of the pool and as I sat, my expectations of the night's sport rose to ridiculous heights. I had the highest hopes and my enthusiasm built within me an almost palpable head of pressure, for which there was no effective safety valve except to fish, yet I knew to start early would only scare the sea trout. When I did wade out to the island below, and move up gingerly from its tip, wading as if creeping in water, I had already seen the first splash in the right bank tail round the island and, using my floating line and two size eight flies, I fished, expecting a pull every cast. I did not get one. I got a splash and nothing else. I fished on. The light was now good and the atmosphere perfect, but I did not get an offer from either left- or right-hand tails. I changed to my slow-sinking line and tried both reaches with this, switching flies at one point to try a larger size on the tail, but again I raised and touched nothing. It was ridiculous. I could see fish in the glides and I would quite honestly have put money on taking several in the conditions.

I had nothing by half past one, and by quarter past two I felt a dead tiredness sweep over me. The head of enthusiasm had turned against me. It had become a column of frustration inside me and it seemed to turn on me and drain my strength. I waded out, walked up the hill to my car, took off my belly waders, feeling bushed, rolled out my sleeping bag and poured myself a cup of tea from my flask. I felt better after the tea. I looked at the sky and felt the mildness of the air.

Conditions were still theoretically superb. I had to try again! I could not abandon the river, on principle, on such a night, even if ten minutes previously I had given up. I pulled my clammy rubber waders on again (ugh!), lifted my rod and this time walked down to the sandy strand on the right bank from which the first glide beside the island may be fished. I had a sea trout on my first cast, then another, then one came off. In all, in about forty minutes, I had four nice fish and raised and pulled others. It was a very brisk party indeed. When I next looked at the sky it was getting light. This time I did retire, but I pulled off my waders and got into my sleeping bag with a completely different set of feelings. I had four lovely fresh sea trout, the best about two-and-a-half pounds. But just before I fell asleep I wondered about it. What had gone wrong and, secondly, what had gone right? I did not know the answer to either question, despite decades of fishing there. It was some time during the next day that it dawned on me that I might have become successful for that hour late in the night because a batch of new fish had come up into the pool. The explanation fitted and I stored it away in my mind. The facts are that I just did not know why the night had shown such an untypical pattern. I had to be glad, however, that my hunch to begin again had been right.

On the evocative and lovely river Shiel which marks the boundary between Argyll and Inverness-shire something similar but more charismatic happened. It was a June night and I was fishing with a friend from Mull. Our beat was the lower half of that short river and the water height that night virtually dictated that we had only two pools which would fish, Garrison and Captains. Garrison is a long slow pool with an attractive tail called the Green Bank; Captains has a streamy head, a weedy deep middle and a deep, gravelly tail. I began on Garrison and caught nothing. At one in the morning Ian came up from Captains, also blank. As much to relieve the tedium as with any hope of success, we swapped pools. It was drizzling, but that is not a bad thing if the midges will be reasonable. Theoretically, we ought to have taken fish, but the facts were that we had fished hard and touched nothing.

Within twenty minutes I was back up from Captains with two fish, or was it three. The pool had filled with fish. Ian, my colleague, came down and we fished Captains together and in the hour that was left before dawn came and the sea trout went off we had taken fourteen fish between us, the best just over three pounds. It was memorable activity, all the more sweet, because we had both virtually reached the conclusion that the night would be blank.

To have settled the night there, as we normally would, would have been most satisfactory. We sat on the bank, glowing with our success. As we sat, the dawn began to strengthen and, as the light increased, salmon began to show. Ian tied on a size eight Willie Gunn double and tried a lie in the middle of the pool. A salmon rose teasingly to his fly, not touching it, several times. 'Ah, one of those', we said. West coast summer salmon do that. But they sometimes take with a sincerity which stuns you after boiling or bulging or vee-ing at your fly abortively. Ian's salmon had all the charateristics of being a teaser, however. It finally turned away and boiled no more. He became frustrated. A salmon would have capped a wonderful night. He sat down on the bank and at that moment we both thought the night was over. We were both tired. Bed would be welcome. I just thought, however, that I would try a fly over Ian's fish and I tied on an identical Willie Gunn. The salmon took it immediately. I was, I suppose, too busy playing the fish on my sea trout rod for the next ten minutes to wonder what went right. Had there been a significant change in the atmosphere or light? Was it a different fish? I didn't know. I remember Ian commenting in a mixture of styles as I played what he had virtually thought of as his salmon. He netted it and a marvellously fat six and a half pounder was taken at half past three, with the light growing stronger every second.

Fish were still moving, and Ian's blood was up. He decided to try a long line and draw his fly off the glide at the far side of Captains and as if it had been rehearsed, a salmon rose to his fly and showed in a strong lunging take. This was a larger fish than mine and the fight was a thunder and lightning business. It came safely ashore at quarter-to-four, eleven pounds and shining fresh. In the two hours since we had met and commiserated with each other at Garrison, we had had the busiest hour of sea trout fishing we have ever had together and had taken two salmon as dawn broke. It was not just ending the night with a trumpet blast. It was ending the night with the whole brass section blowing *fortissimo*.

The bank of a sea trout river at night is like a different country, no matter how well you have known it during the day. This is partly because our perception of it changes with the loss of the light. The loss of light is not total. No phase of the night and no night of the year is totally dark. Even in the most pit-mirk hour of the darkest night there is always something which distinguishes black from black, as if the earth itself had a photon or two of light to lend us. The sense of smell seems enhanced at night. Walking through a wood, one can sometimes smell bands of scent from different trees and bushes. Sudden pools of perfume can arrest you. I have been stopped in my tracks in early June by the scent of an unseen hawthorn in bloom. Perfumes clothe the banks at night in a way absent or unnoticed when our eyes dominate.

Sounds at night can also take on a heightened sigificance. I have at least one nervous friend who cannot tolerate the noises of the night and who retires from the river nervous and alarmed. There are certainly some unusual happenings on the banks at night. Resting cattle may be disturbed and rise with much blowing and snorting, as indeed we would if they happened to disturb us in bed. There are strange cries from bankside animals. Night birds call. Occasionally unseen dramas are worked out, leaving it to our imagination to explain what the disturbance is all about. It is interesting how the imagination urgently, sometimes frantically, tries to clothe sounds with rational explanations. Two of us once approached a quiet, deep pool on the Shiel and were alarmed to hear an amazing splashing in the rushes. It sounded like poachers and in that still dark night the unexplained disturbance made the hair on the neck stiffen. It turned out to be an otter subduing a thrashing sea trout among the reeds. Relief, almost joy, followed that discovery. It is the unexplained event which frightens most.

I was alone one night on the Shiel, fishing a pool called Heathery Bank and I was well tucked in by the water when I heard voices. I heard dimly at first, then clearly, two men deep in conversation. They were talking about people they had just met. It was half-past-one in the morning and apart from their voices, the riverside had been totally quiet, almost sullen. I could not see the speakers, but their voices approached and I was eventually aware of their footsteps. They were walking in the deep darkness down a not-too-easy path, but there was never the sound of a stumble, never a comment about footing or where they were going and never the glint of a torch. They talked continuously and amicably, as friends might on a stroll. I know that path well. It takes me down to the Duck Pond pool and into the fields beyond where Cliff begins. I stood still where I was and the conversing night walkers passed me by a yard or so away. I could not see them from where I was and they were unaware of me by the river. Who were they? Where were they going? Why were they walking through the dark woods in the small hours of the night, deep in genial conversation? I could not explain it. Above all, how did they know the woods so well that not a syllable of their talk was misplaced as they ambled on in the dark? Their voices dwindled after they passed me. Whether they took the rough path down to Duck Pond, or knew a track up through the woods to the road above, I do not know. For me they were just the Amiable Talkers of the Night. After they passed, the river settled again to its dourness and silence descended, broken only by the sound of my casting.

Wading a river at night can be alarming even when you reassure yourself that there are few hazards and when you have waded the route by day a score of times. Water in the dark takes on a leaden quality. Distances exaggerate themselves. Landmarks on the bank distort or disappear and it is easy to become disorientated. Once or twice on long wades to fish a glide near the far bank on the Spey or the Dee I have found myself playing fish which circled me in the black water and I have turned round and round with them and have lost, for a moment, my sense of direction. But in the isolation of wading like this and in the feeling of searching for the lurking fish in glides under the far bank there is a wonderful sense of mystery. This sense is never far away in night sea trout fishing. Darkness and stillness release the mind from being in thrall to the eyes. The rod and line feel different in your hand and there is a momentous expectancy as you cast out and pull your flies off the glide under the bushes on the far bank, hoping to feel the pull of a sea trout. Sometimes there is a vestige of the visual as a sea trout takes and produces a little mark like a silver line on the surface in the rise. More often the take is only signalled to your fingers on the line and your hand on the rod. Where possible, I net fish where I am standing, slip them into the bag on my back and fish on. Only a big one would make me wade out. On the Dee one evening, I hooked a very lively salmon on my sea trout fly and found I had left my net in the car. It was parked on the grass some way behind me. I waded out when the fish was quiet and giving line, walked to the Volvo and still playing the fish, raised the tailgate, reached for the net and suddenly found myself playing a salmon a long way off which had wakened up and was making the most astonishing fast run. I retraced my steps, but armed with the net this time and eventually brought the fish ashore. On another occasion, a fish of about four pounds broke through the bottom of my landing net and I was left wading somewhere out in the grey river with the fish making off through the torn net and I was left playing it with my rod in one hand and the net in the other, held up like an idiot's handmirror, to let the line run through it as the fish made off. Totally bizarre! I lost that fish, after a most interesting, private cabaret in the dark.

I have never actually lost my way in the river at night, but I have sometimes made some curious mistakes of judgement. Usually these relate to mistaking the best way to wade out and finding that I had to fight my way out through a rhododendron bush or worse. It can work the other way too. A mistake in the dark can be quite productive. Once, on an unfamiliar beat of the Border Esk, I fished down to the tail of the pool and found a glide which I liked below some trees. It was very gloomy and I cast well over to this seemingly choice piece of water and felt strongly that there must be a fish in it. I imagined it as a slow, deep glide. I took a fish, then another and then pulled a third and, in brief, had a rather productive time. I returned the following day to look at that glide and I couldn't see it. There was a piece of water there, but it was only inches deep. How could it have held sea trout? That remains in my mind as an example of the night presenting me with a fishable piece of water which the day would have scorned. Had

I planned my wading and fishing carefully in daylight, I would not have bothered fishing there. Sea trout inhabit rivers at night as if they were different waters. They move into runs and glides and, particularly tails of pools which would seem incapable of holding them by day. So do salmon. In the dusk on the Dee I am always too keen to wade, when experience has shown that the salmon move into water no more than knee deep, right under our feet on the bankside path.

The night river is a different place from the day river, and the fish inhabit its water differently. They take on a night character, as the bankside birds and animals do. The best sea trout fishers change too as they fish into the dark. They identify with the changes, and in a way, blend with them into the night. Those fishers who try to fish as they would by day are likely to be unsuccessful and frustrated. Anglers who are always turning on lamps, always calling to their friends, always trying to see their cast in the air above them, rather than feel it, are fighting the darkness. To do well for sea trout at night the darkness must be your ally and friend. You must somehow understand it and the best way to this is, psychologically, to blend with the night river itself. Identifying well has its rewards. You find, in the night river, excitement there, not anxiety. There is intrigue and mystery there, not menace. In the night sea trout there is a wild elusive quarry, almost untemptable by day in the low summer river, but a strong and often willing taker in the dusk and dark. Sometimes, when day fishing for trout or salmon is slow, I play a kind of game and shut my eyes and imagine that it is the night. When I do this, succeeding, as it were in a kind of meditation, the rod in my hand changes. My fingers become more intelligent as they move the line in through the water. If I can sustain the illusion, I sometimes manage to slow down my day fishing and invest it with some of the qualities of the night. Sometimes I hook a trout like this, by willing the river, as it were, to take on its night style. 'Thinking dark' is a way of becoming more intimate with the water and becoming more sensitive to the line and the rod and the flies. But one's eyes always want to be boss. The lamp of the body shines on the river and tries to dominate it, telling the hand to do this, search out there, speed up now, or hang the fly there. The eye can be a tyrant, and sometimes is the worst adviser possible. This is one of the lessons learned and re-learned at night. We have other senses and other ways of relating to the river and its fish. Only in darkness can these be fully realised. This is the message of the night.

CHAPTER
5

The road to Fionn

IN A STRIKING WAY, Highland and Hebridean rivers draw together and unify the glens they run through. They form a focus for the landscape and with a kind of natural magnetism, they seem to embrace their surroundings, bringing the glens into being. I have often felt these waters winding me in as I walk and fish. I am drawn to paths by the river when the more obvious route should be more direct. Fishers know this scenario well. You walk, and cast a fly here and there, lured by this stream and that glassy glide, all somehow irresistible. It is a form of seduction, waylaying you as you head for pools and lochs above. Walking and fishing a West Highland glen like this makes you aware of the unity of the whole system. You are always conscious of the lochs in the moor above and you can feel the river tapping its water from the mosses, gathering the hill burns as it flows, and forging the final link with the sea below. As you fish, you are drawn in to be part of the system too. Like the landscape, you also find the river no mere contingency of the valley; it is its *raison d'être*.

Like many fishers, I have a deep, imaginative attachment to many of the Highland waters I fish, or hope to fish. I dream about remote glens which promise wilderness reaches where pools, seldom fished, harbour trout and salmon lurking in their depths in a primeval way. Rivers flowing from large lochs above, hint at these hidden waters, lying below visible high tops, but secret. I have to confess that these lochs, and the high glens of rivers which drain them, form landscapes in my mind which can be the object of the deepest longings and the richest imaginings. Paradoxically, these waters can be both the practical objective of a fishing journey and yet have the qualities of a land of lost content. This mixture of practicality and nostalgia is fundamental to Highland and Hebridean fishing. The waters symbolise much that is yearned for, achievable, and yet lost. It is not surprising that such places can achieve something of the status of a personal myth.

I developed such a longing for the Fionn Loch. I first heard about its
character from a friend on Loch Maree when I fished that water many
years ago. He was the late Charlie McLaren, born and brought up in
Kinlochewe, and one of the most outstanding fishers and men of the
Highlands I have met. While we were drifting and fishing Maree, he
indicated where Fionn lay, pointing north from the water at
Kinlochewe, and his arm swept along a formidable range of hills –
Slioch and all the Letterewe summits, looking magnificent, but impenetrable. Fionn lay there, eight or nine miles long, I was told, full of bays
which reach into the surrounding hills, full of trout, many of which
were large, and here and there holding a salmon which had run up the
Little Gruinard river. It was a marvellous picture. It worked on my
mind and became a kind of symbol for me of all that was remote and
beautiful in the West Highlands, a kind of pocket wilderness, isolated,
beautiful and unspoiled. With its glen below where the Little Gruinard
flowed, it became a place of longing and I fervently hoped to be able to
reach it some day and fish it.

It was almost thirty years later that I had the chance to fish the Little
Gruinard and put my foot, as it were, on the Road to Fionn. Why did I
wait so long? I don't really know. I could blame other fishing. I could
blame work, lack of time or even pursuing other dreams. When the
offer came, however, there was a feeling of inevitability about it.
A close fishing friend, Ian, telephoned me to say that he had taken
September fishings on the Little Gruinard and he asked me to join the
party. We lived in a white cottage at the mouth of the river, looking out
to Gruinard Bay and each day we walked up the glen to fish. We could
go as far as we liked back into the hills – fishing the river, its side lochs
and, if we wanted to, fishing Fionn. In practical terms, without sleeping out, fishing Fionn involved spending more time walking than
fishing and rather than lose fishing time on the river below, no
members of the fishing team had actually reached the loch. The day
realistically offered a maximum of eight hours walking and fishing.

I set out on the first day to walk the river, fishing here and there, and
to try also to reach Fionn. I walked with Andrew who knew the river
well. The first two or three miles of rough path takes you up beside a
pounding rocky river with salmon pools and fast streams and pots, then
the foaming gorge and, above it, in moorland stillness, the lower flats.
A couple of miles further over grass and heather takes you beside rocky
pools, other gently flowing flats, then an alternation of stony runs and
pools, some with rowan or birch clinging to boulders, some with
stepped white rapids up the gradients. That first day had the character
of an introduction. Andrew named the pools as we walked, stopping to
introduce this stream and that glide, and, rather as if shaking hands,
I fished each briefly, then walking on we scanned the upper valley for

signs of the loch. Although he had fished the Little Gruinard several times, he had never actually reached Fionn itself.

About six miles up the valley the river changes character radically; you get the first sight of a loch ahead. You expect it to be Fionn, but it is not. On that first day's walking I fervently wished it had been, because, having cast a fly here and a fly there as I walked I was running out of time. The loch water we saw, and shortly reached was called the first salmon pool, and its name is deceiving. It is neither first, nor is it a pool, but is a loch of more than quarter of a mile in length, cliffy at its head where the stream comes in and drawing off into a bay at the lower end where the Gruinard picks up speed and plunges into salmon pools and runs below.

Andrew left me there to try some of the pools immediately below. I stood by the glide where the still water became a river again and drew off into the fast water below and thought it looked perfect for a salmon. The broad waters of the lochan gathered there, picking up speed. I wondered if there was any depth, but the light prevented me from seeing clearly into the water. In the glide, under the shadow of a large rock on the far side, I thought I saw boulders, but the light on the surface frustrated any further knowledge of it. I decided to let my fly explore it – a smallish black hair wing with a gold body which I had tied up. My eleven-foot sea trout rod had a neutral line on it, but I had spliced on a sinking, braided leader which I had been experimenting with in places I wanted to keep the line up and let a small fly go down. The glide in front of me needed a longish line out to cover it, and I felt some urgency to put the fly into the area of water near the far side where the shadow of a cliffy boulder darkened the water and promised to let me see in.

Towards the end of the glide my line checked and I tightened and felt the fly catching on a boulder. I released the fly and cast out again and this time it checked at almost the same place. I raised the rod and felt the pulse of a salmon. Marvellous! I backed out of the water, trying to get the fish to follow me up into the clearer waters of the loch above and it came nicely. It ran up, then turned and ran towards me and again turned and ran back towards its original lie. This happened twice and once I was able to see the fish, a coloured small salmon perhaps five pounds in weight. That was the last I saw of it. My braided leader parted at the loop moments afterwards. It does not really help to say that I would certainly have returned the fish. What annoyed me was a tackle failure like this. That leader had seemed sound. It had been used for some hard fishing immediately prior to the Little Gruinard and had done well. Perhaps that was it. Perhaps I had not looked carefully enough at the loop-to-loop link with my cast. It seemed that the top loop had chafed through, or perhaps had struck a boulder. Anyway, the fish was gone.

I walked upstream alone after losing the fish, came to the streams at the head and saw, reaching away about a mile before me, the rippled waters of what looked like an arm of Fionn proper. In the distance, at narrows, it seemed to turn south behind a headland. I imagined the body of the great loch lying there, stretched out among the hills. Once again, the draw-off of the loch was what attracted my attention. This time it was deep, slow and rocky, but in addition to the gliding pace of the water, the reach had a good wave on it. I had repaired the leader, attached a similar black and gold fly and two or three casts later, felt, not a check to the fly, but a sharp knock and I was into a fish which pulled up into the deep water of the loch above. It might be a salmon, but there was something less pulsing about the feel. It was heavy and strong, but not thrusting in the way a salmon might be. It took a few minutes to get the fish in towards the boulders on which I was standing. There was deep clear water in front, six or eight feet of it. This allowed me to see the fish and I think I was, by that time, not expecting it to be a salmon. It was a big trout and, as I brought it with difficulty to a precarious bay among the rocks – the only place in which I might beach it – I saw it in the water below me, a great spotted fish, a brown trout, the first fruits of Fionn, I thought. I got it ashore with a feeling of great success, and decided to take it home, partly because it was the best Scottish Highland loch trout I had ever taken. The colour was impressive when I killed the fish, brown on the back, yellow on the flanks, with well marked spots, but the fish was slightly black under the gills. Well, it was September. I took it and photographed it on a rock. It was a fat fish, but with rather odd fins. Its tail was worn, like a tank-bred fish. But surely that couldn't be? It must just be an old fish. After all, it was three-and-a-half pounds. It was a real Fionn trout, I told myself, perhaps a *ferox*, but even as I was telling myself this I felt doubts about it. The story just wasn't right. This was not the right kind of trout for the setting.

I turned for home, met Andrew and showed him the fish, then met Hamish, one of the estate owners at that time and described to him how I had taken this heavy trout in Fionn. He was quick to say two things. First that he had never seen a trout of that size from the river and secondly, that I had not taken it in Fionn, but on the second salmon pool. Fionn lay well above that. So I had deluded myself. I had not reached Fionn at all. There was no time to explore further that day, so, walking and stopping to fish the odd pool, we set off for home. When I got there, I laid out my fish on the slab in the outhouse but my fish had changed colour. It now did not look like a brown trout at all. It had turned into a rather grey sea trout. But the fins? Looking carefully at it. There could be little doubt that my fish, taken ironically in a remote, natural, unstocked water, was a cage bred and fed fish. It had all

the marks of it – a fat full body, with poor fins. Its tail was
especially disappointing, being rounded instead of square, not fully
developed, as if the fish were trying to re-absorb it. Nobody could tell
me where sea trout were bred in the area. Salmon farms existed in the
sea within a few miles of the river, but no sea trout were being bred
there, I was assured. I knew of one experiment with sea trout reared in
cages, but that was on Loch Eilt, many miles to the south, absolutely
out of range. The mystery remains, and with it the wry notion that
Fionn seemed to have a sense of irony towards me. I had longed for the
loch, imagining it as an unspoiled, wild place, as indeed it is. Yet it had
eluded me and instead of the catch I had hoped for as a reward for
reaching a wilderness paradise after an arduous walk, it had rewarded
me with what could almost be described as a man-made fish.

The following day I was stiff and foot weary and I elected to try the
easier option; I fished for salmon and sea trout on the lower and middle
river. It was a day of seeing fish, pulling them, getting short contact
only and landing just two finnock, which were duly returned. I thought
my hand had lost its cunning. I lost a salmon in the tail of the Garden
Pool, pulled one hard in Harry's Run below, had plucks and stops here
and there as I worked my way up the river, but really, apart from
raising my own temperature, did badly. The extraordinary thing was
that the three other rods in our party, distributed over the lower and
middle river, all came home with long faces; they had all touched fish,
hooked fish and lost fish. The Little Gruinard has many reaches of fast
stony water where salmon lie in pockets and where takes are sudden
fast plucks at the fly as it sweeps past. It is demanding fishing, arduous
wading and walking and a challenge to hand and eye in accurate casting
and fly presentation. The easier water is the flats where slowish deep
pools are formed in the moor, but even in these, despite fish showing
in most of the lies, there were no catches to report. That day illustrated
a basic rule of fishing – that failure is marginally tolerable if it is
universally suffered.

It was clear from a study of the map and discussions with Hamish
that I had really taken the wrong road to Fionn. I had, logically as
I thought, followed the river all the way. The right way to go was to
ford the river at the bottom of the first salmon pool, roughly where
I had lost the salmon in the glide, and strike out south east over the
moor and, in about half an hour, I would reach an arm of Fionn and
from there I could work my way along the shore, fishing as I went.
I took my belly waders in a backpack and set out. It took two hours to
reach the lower salmon pool, stopping only once to fish the Upper Flats
because I saw two most lovely head-and-tail rises there on still water,
but neither showed any interest in my fly in the glassy conditions. It
was like fishing in the sky, since the clouds and the banks above were

perfectly reflected in the pool. I was now, once again, at
the lower salmon pool and, donning my waders, I fished the glide
again, before attempting to ford it, but nothing moved to the fly.
Thinking that it was the best place to cross, I collected up my stuff,
hitching my pack as high on my back as it would go, and started in.
When I had fished it two days previously, the glide had looked shallow
in places, almost too shallow to fish. Now that I was wading it, however, I saw what a mistake I had made. The glide was very deep, six
feet or more, with enormous boulders in it. What I had thought was
the bottom was in fact the tops of huge rocks. It was impossible. I had
to retreat and find a way across the river lower down. For a small river,
the Little Gruinard is difficult to wade. Its bed is a mass of boulders.
Streams shift the shingle and form sudden potholes. Wading it illustrated well the sound principle, 'Prod first and wade after'. Using a stick
I did that and struck out over the moor for the hidden arm of Fionn.

Fionn lay unseen until the last shoulder, then seemed to pull up into
sight. Fionn revealed! A long arm of water was backed by steep hills to
the east running down to a shoreline where huge rocks lay in profusion.
At the head, lying just below me as I walked down, was a beautiful
sandy bay sweeping round the end of the arm in a golden arc. Fionn
reached to the south beyond the long arm and in the main body of the
loch I could see promontories, rocks in shallow bays, and in the distance, the slopes of Meall Mheinnidh and Beinn Lair – two of the
Letterewe heights. Fionn at last! As if to welcome me, the clouds over
the hills at the southern end, over eight miles away, parted and the sun
shone on the slopes. It would have been marvellous to keep going and
reach the far end, but that was well beyond walking range for one day.
Besides, I wanted to fish Fionn. I set up my trout rod with a cast of two
flies, and fished the rocky shore and the first trout to come to me was
small. Then, wading round the great sandy bay I had two, one fully
three-quarters of a pound, which I took and one which I returned. On
the rocks beyond the bay, after finding it difficult to wade because of
the huge boulders, I first saw, then raised and hooked a splendid fish,
which pulled very hard and broke loose. It was a substantial trout.
These Fionn fish, taken over the sand were beautiful – yellow and white
on the belly, hard and well shaped and beautifully spotted. I did not
have much time to spend in that lovely bay, so, taking in its solitude
and perfect configuration, where wind and wave had shaped that
crescent of golden sand backed by the moor, I got up to go. Acting on
impulse, I bent down and wrote my name on the sand. I felt I had to
record actually getting to Fionn, even if the record would not last
longer than the first high wave. I didn't really mind Fionn wiping it
out. It reminded me that I was the temporary feature of the place, the
intruder, while Fionn itself was the continuing presence.

Walking and wading round the point was not possible in the time, so I struck out across the headland to the west and planned to strike the western arm of Fionn where the Little Gruinard flowed out. Aird Dhubh was moorland with low hills and a mass of lochs. I cast my fly over several but raised nothing. But I had to remind myself that I was walking to the western arm of Fionn, and not spending the day trying for hill trout in the process. It was a weaving route, avoiding lochs, choosing the best way over bogs and getting views of Fionn to my left as I crossed the higher ridges. The loch opened out to the south, showing what looked like an island with old pine trees and on the south western shore, what must have been the house marked on the map sandwiched between an island, Eiuch Bhain, and a sinisterly named area, Bad Bog. When I reached Fionn again I saw the track on the other bank which runs from Aultbea over the moor. I had asked about that track and was told it was a two-land-rover road – one constantly available to winch the other out of the bog. A couple of boats lay on the shore there, little used, I thought, if it required all day to get to them before fishing. I fished down the lower bays towards the point where the river drew off and had another lovely trout just under a pound, which made my bag a couple. I carefully fished the river bay for salmon, but touched none. The water looked perfect for salmon there. One of my hill walking friends who had in past years walked over to Fionn from Kinlochewe, camping out on the way, told of mounting his trout rod and fishing one of the remote bays of Fionn and taking a salmon, one of the best remembered surprises of his hill walking.

I had no luck with salmon on that occasion, neither on the loch nor the fascinating streams and lochans below between Fionn and the two loch-like salmon pools I have already described. I fished these carefully, but again saw nothing. The reaches below Fionn are marvellous places, with banks of fresh heather, red-berried rowan trees clinging to precipitous banks, and pools which vary from streams among rocks to black lochans with cliffy banks. Grouse show here and there; sea birds fly over; occasional trout ring the surface of the lochans. In this unspoiled place, I expected somewhere to see a salmon, or better still, to hook one. Every pool promised it, but nothing happened. Perhaps this is an important message of the wild; salmon are their own unpredictable, fitful selves, even where they are seldom fished. Salmon may behave like fools for a week after reaching fresh water, but thereafter, they are difficult, sometimes exasperating fish. It was not that I felt salmon ought to have taken my fly that day; – there is no *ought* in salmon fishing. It was that the hooking of a salmon in such a place would have been deeply satisfying.

I had almost completed the circle from where I had forded the river three hours before. Now, fishing and walking down the banks of both salmon pools – where I could actually get down the steep sides of the south bank and reach the water, I found myself again at the glide where I had lost the fish on the first day. From the south bank the glide did not look very fishable. I tried it, but the flies did not swing round well. I soon tired of it, wound up and walked down the right bank of the Little Gruinard for three-quarters of an hour before seeing Andrew fishing down the Upper Flats where fish were showing from time to time, heading and tailing or splashing. He was frustrated. He had seen fish all day and none had even moved to his flies. I walked on, feeling by this time a little leg-weary. I tried the Middle Flats, particularly the tail and the glides below where I saw two fish, both coloured, but nothing came, then the Pulpit where the rock which gives it its name was draped in purple heather as if for Passion Sunday. I took nothing but a small trout which I returned. I looked long at the Upper Gorge pool, wondering if I had the energy to fish it, when a salmon showed and I found I had plenty, but, like all the others I had seen and fished over that day, it ignored my flies in water which looked perfect. Andrew arrived and decided to rest the Gorge and try it again. I left him to it. I passed Bob on the Lower Gorge working his way down to Major's and Tattersall's. Ian was working the streams there too. I was tottering on heading for the cottage, having walked the best part of fourteen miles, a fair bit of it in breast waders.

When I got home, and had a cup of tea and the others began to trickle down from the river, each with their stories. Bob said that as soon as I had passed he had got into a fish and lost it after a struggle in the maelstrom of the Lower Gorge. Ian had had a terrific battle with a red fish in fast streamy water above Tattersalls. It too had escaped. Bob moved another above the Peat Pool. They said conditions had suddenly improved after I passed. I would like to have been able to claim that I was a beneficial influence, that Fionn had charmed me in some way and I had passed it on, but the facts were that none of the fish had actually been landed, so I said nothing.

The Little Gruinard and Fionn represent a special kind of fishing unit in Scotland. It is a whole loch and river system, now, after a change of ownership, owned by one estate. The river and loch have the great virtue of being isolated enough to be in a completely unspoiled state. It is one of a very few systems where a whole salmon river and its lochs and spawning streams and the whole delicate environment might be carefully studied. It is a wonderful unspoiled unity of river, loch and hill. The new owner of the estate already owned half of the system, and now that he can manage the whole Little Gruinard – Fionn watershed, he has established what is one of the first conservation and restraint programmes in Scotland, coupled with research, which he has helped to fund. He has arranged for his tenants to photograph, measure and weigh the salmon they catch, and return them to the river. I hope the new owner in his enthusiasm for this research will also allow anglers to take one or two for the pot, measured and recorded, of course. The opportunity to carry out research on a whole small system like this is unique. From a research point of view, the programme is a most enlightened one, deeply respecting the unspoiled environment of Fionn and Gruinard, yet allowing responsible access and careful fishing.

In a way, conservation and restraint, instead of restricting the merit of a river, actually emphasise what sporting fishing is about. It is not about corpses of fish, although the triumph and delight one feels in taking a well-shaped, silver fish home for the table is unforgettable. Fishing, however, is about sport. It is about places with atmosphere; it is about wild and often uncatchable fish; it is about skills of hand and eye and it is in a very important way about involvement with the environment. For me, the package needs contact with fish, but it does not need the car boot full to show the sport I have had. Conservation and environmental research should not, in my view, go as far as refusing fishing access. Nor should it prevent anglers taking a fish home for the table. I feel in my bones, however, that the whole tone of game fishing is likely to alter in the final years of this century. It is likely to become a sport more conscious of the environment than ever before, and more responsible in its use of natural resources than formerly. We cannot pretend to be lovers of the salmon and its wilderness rivers if all we want to do is crop the fish out, by angling or by netting. The tide has turned against salt water netting now, and this means that there will be, we hope, more salmon returning miraculously from the oceans to our rivers. It also means, however, that fishers must now act with the greatest responsibility in the way they fish. We are not plunderers of nature. Quite the reverse; anglers are its lovers. We do not set out to kill the thing we love; we set out to be challenged by it, to study it and to nurture it. Yet, in conservation we are still anglers, still in some sense hunters and killers. The paradox is that by being so, we are also the most highly motivated conservators.

I think, if I had managed to get to Fionn as a young angler, thirty years before I actually cast my fly on its waters, I might have felt that it was a system where the profligacy of nature would ensure that all I killed would be replaced, and more. Now I see it as a lovely, fragile place, where the most favoured elements of the Highlands come together to produce a profoundly meaningful environment with an almost mystical unity to it. My delight in Fionn is not mere contemplation, however. I want deeply to be not only an observer of its glory but also an actor in it. Fishing is a relevant action in a Highland glen. It is homage, not betrayal. This is only true, however, if it is done responsibly, and that, for me, is the key to rare places like Fionn. The first tales of Fionn fired my imagination, and, many years later the experience of it seemed to kindle something deeper in me than just filling my bag there. The road to Fionn has become, for me, not only a memorable journey of the greatest fishing interest but also an experience of the spirit. It feels at one level like a journey richly suffused with a mixture of homage and humility inspired by the place. I have to confess, however, that I also feel some disquiet. I feel about Fionn what I feel about other vulnerable and rare things; I feel anxiety, even fear, that without insight we will allow ourselves to destroy its essences; we will preside over its decadence. This message applies to many other places we fish now. There is an ultimatum before us: we either approach them in an enlightened way or we risk destroying them. The paradox of using but preserving the wilderness we love is raised universally, as it was with great particularity on the road to Fionn. Only the right balance can resolve it.

CHAPTER
6

Deeside in May

THERE IS A SENSE in which we are always trying to turn our salmon into trout, and there is a way in which, each spring and summer, the fish obligingly respond. I do not mean that a biological transformation takes place; I mean that, as the spring warms up, salmon begin to be interested in small flies, swum like natural nymphs up near the surface of the water and in taking them, they can look like trout. This can be dramatic. Fish of ten, fifteen or twenty pounds rising to small flies and showing as they do is one of the great spectacles of salmon fishing and can lead to that most satisfied of all remarks in reporting a success, 'He rose just like a trout – head, back, tail – and I was into him'.

A behavioural change of this order is itself interesting. It is as if the spring river makes the salmon want to be a parr again. In colder waters, when the fish has to be sought out with sunk lines and deeply fished flies, it behaves like an ocean fish. That is thrilling enough, but when a fish as long as your arm rises to a fly as though it were a fingerling again, we are into magical territory. It is also magical, and like most magic, faintly ludicrous, that a fish which does not feed while it is in the river, should want to take a small fly – a speck, a mote, perhaps no more than half-an-inch of sparse hair. I could go on in incredulity. For instance, we have no evidence that the salmon takes any other kind of foreign object except the angler's lures or flies when it is in fresh water. Indeed, we have very little evidence that the salmon takes *natural* bodies in its freshwater sojourn. We do not often see salmon rising to natural flies, although one or two observers have noted it. Frank Sawyer, writing about nymphs on chalk streams suggests that salmon occasionally take take them. A.H.E. Wood, writing in Eric Taverner's *Lonsdale Salmon Fishing*, describes in detail how the sight of Irish salmon below an eel weir in summer rising to moths made him change his fly fishing tactics. He quite simply found a white moth wet trout fly, and fished it, dibbling it at first, and taking six fish on this approach in his first day. He went on to discover that greasing his line helped with the presentation of the fly. That was 1903, and was the birth of floating line fishing for salmon. I am glad to say fly fishing has not been the same since.

I am so attracted to fishing salmon with a floating line and a small fly that I try it out in my impatience from March or early April onwards. Perhaps my earliest efforts are not really full floating line approaches, but they are pre-echoes of it. I use a neutral line in the early spring, which rides in the surface of the water rather than on it, and I may use something like a one-inch tube fly, or a size six which I dress on a long-shanked, light treble. On the Dee in late April and May, fishing a full floating line and, say, a lightly dressed eight or ten Stoat's Tail is a great delight. I cast a longish line, say twenty-five yards or more. I mend it to compensate for the vagaries of the stream, then, having done that I let the stream pull the line and fly round at its own speed, presenting the fly just below the surface. I cannot, perhaps communicate exactly what this delectable form of salmon fishing feels like, practised in the glow of an early week in May when late daffodils and spring broom dress the banks, under the small new birch leaves. This fishing is often like a kind of writing, letting the long line gently open out in the flow as a question mark might, becoming in the process a curve, then a long straight line sliding through the stream at forty-five degrees below you. At the end of the sweep as the cast fishes round, I have sometimes thought of the floating line hovering below me – line, cast and fly – as a kind of incipient exclamation mark – waiting for the moment of the take which would energise it. It is a dreamy notion – the question mark and the exclamation, written on water with a floating line.

Salmon fishing, for me, is often enhanced by its metaphors. I like the idea of writing on the stream. Think also of the idea of 'dwelling on the fly' – letting it unroll steadily without jerks or twitches and letting it hang for a long second or two before re-casting, an excellent tactic sustained by the effect of the rod 'dwelling'. There are other figures too. Some talk of hanging the fly; others of sweeping it slowly round, edging it gently over the lie, dangling it, holding it, swimming it. The images are endless. They are all indices of persistence and steadiness in covering the water at the right speed and depth. Covering a spring pool in the right way might seem to a casual observer to be a form of indolence. They should not allow the appearance to delude them. Dwelling on the fly and hanging it long in spring glides is very far from this; it is thinly disguised excitement. It is passion restrained. I know something of what goes on in my own hand and in my head as I swing the fly round over the spring Dee at Aboyne, expecting a take every yard. My hand is consciously stilled, but my head is racing with language – reports, accounts, dialogues, theories, quotations – some of it history, some theory and some plain hope. In a way this mental flow acts as a kind of diversionary tactic. It quells the urgent and passionate energy which I feel, and in doing so, helps me to be successful. In May, on the Dee this quite simply means that the images in my head help me to hold my hand and let the floating line write its message on the water. It is a tactic of being restrained enough to let the fly search, giving the fish time to rise, take the fly, turn away and produce that glorious draw which signals that you are into him!

Fishing floating line or a neutral as I describe, I have often taken my first fish well before May, often before the leaves show on the riverside. For example, I have taken a fish in the first week of April on Lower Birgham on Tweed when only the poplars showed touches of green and the flower, but not the leaf, was on the blackthorn. I had had a dialogue with myself that day, with the ghillie prompting, about whether to fish the neutral line or the sinker, for the air was cold and the sun lit rather than heated the day. I won, as it were. I fished the neutral, and attached a one-inch light copper tube to my cast which probably fished six inches down in the stream. Long casts covered the water at the Otter Rock, but nothing came. We were almost at our march below when the fish took. A long draw on the line and then a pull which took five yards of line off the open reel. I did not see that take, even if it was just slightly below the surface. It was a lovely fish, eight pounds, and when I brought it ashore I felt exultant. The year had turned and a new season of floating line fishing was confirmed. I felt like shouting to the trees and bushes on the banks, 'It's all right! You can flower now, for the fish are coming up to the fly at the surface'.

For about twelve years prior to writing this I have been lucky enough to fish the Dee at Aboyne in the first full week of May. I need hardly describe the glory of that time on Deeside. The gorse and broom on the banks are brilliant yellow. The birches and the willows are marvellous, fresh green. The last of the daffodils and primroses are still showing and the new grass and growing crops carpet the fields. Through this the Dee flows, still full with the water from the snows of the Cairngorms – clear, glittering, pure. The sunlight and the clarity of the water can give you the illusion that the shingle and boulder bottom is only knee-deep. It can be difficult to believe that water of such clarity and light could conceal salmon, yet salmon lie in scores in the streams and pools and a trained eye can see some of them. You can spot them in the air, of course. They show. They splash and dimple; they lunge; they boil. In the first week of May, middle Dee can be full of fish and its pools can draw from you a depth of urgency to cover them which is hard to explain to non-anglers. It is as though your thoughts and desires and energies were all focused on one compelling goal. In the Border ballads and folk stories there is a similar theme – that of a man who hears the music of the underworld – the pipes of Elfland – and he is irresistibly drawn towards it and goes through a door in the hillside into a different existence. It is not putting too much into salmon fishing in May to say that it is similar to that. Indeed, I would go further. Those who were seduced by the faery music left the world and died in a kind of ecstasy. Salmon fishers go through something like this, but come back, and describe it, and share it. It is a magnificent compulsion, never better experienced than in fishing the Dee in May with a floating line.

There is a tradition of morning and evening fishing being the productive times in May. On the Dee this may be as much connected with the direction of the sunlight than anything else. The river flows virtually west–east, flowing from the Cairngorms more or less directly to the North Sea at Aberdeen. On a dull day it does not matter much where the sun is, but in the bright weather we often see in May, it is important that the pools are lit from the tails in the morning, and a bright afternoon with sun in the eyes of the fish is least productive. I do not think salmon are afraid of the light itself. Salmon are, after all, fish which swim near the surface of the sea during their sea feeding phase and in fresh water will usually choose a lie between two and five feet deep. In lochs they settle near the edge or round sunk rocks, off points and along sunken reefs. They are not light shy, but they have difficulty, as other fish have, in seeing into glittering sunlight. On lochs I hate the sun being in the eye of the wind – that is, shining from the same direction – because fish feed into the wind and are blinded by the glare. On rivers salmon face the flow. A downstream sun blots out most of the detail and a small fly, fished near the glittering surface, would be lost. I have sometimes surprised myself by taking fish on bright afternoons on the Dee, but I believe that what happens is that the fish, sensing the passage of the fly, turns after it, and immediately gets better sighting conditions. There is another drawback of bright downstream sun, however. The shadow of the line, cast and fly precede the fly itself and disturb fish.

The way salmon move to the fly in the daytime on Dee is different from the quieter rises of the evening. Some fish will show like trout, breaking the surface with their backs. Others will show a head, or a nose. Some will boil and seem to suck the fly down. In some pools, especially where the angler is slightly above the fish, say on rocks or a high bank, the whole rise can be seen in detail. On the Dee, the ghillie at Aboyne often sits on the bank just below the angler and watches the fly coming round and gets a good view of the take, or the mis-take. A ghillie who calls to say a fish is following, or is rising to the fly is no friend. Most anglers would tense at his words and almost certainly pull

Fly fishing beat five, Helmsdale, February

Kildonan Falls in Flood, Helmsdale

On the Foam Pool, River Helmsdale

Sunset, head of Upper Torrish, River Helmsdale

The ultimate February reward, – a 9 lb Helmsdale springer

The Doon, Smithston: fishing the Scoot Hole

A sea trout, Loch Ba, Mull

An early May sea trout from the Dee

The Little Gruinard, Wester Ross

A loch-like pool on the Little Gruinard, near Loch Fionn

Glimmering in the distance, Loch Fionn, Wester Ross

On the road to Fionn, fishers stop on the hill for lunch

The two loch-like salmon pools on the upper Little Gruinard

A superb, fresh-run May ten-pounder from the Dee

Into a strong fish on a glide on the Dee at Aboyne

Quietly searching for a summer salmon, tail of the Lang Pool, River Doon

On the Jetty Pool, May, River Dee, Aboyne

Casting a floating line over the Lummels in May, River Dee, Aboyne

Wading the Holandsay Pool, River Namsen, Norway – a pool famous for its very large salmon

On the Lower Irrigation Pool, River Dee, Aboyne

On the Namsen, Norway

Wading the head of the Red Rock, River Dee, Aboyne

A catch of Dee salmon on small wispy hair wing flies

A collection of waddingtons and toshes contrasted with a box of small summer drury flies and doubles

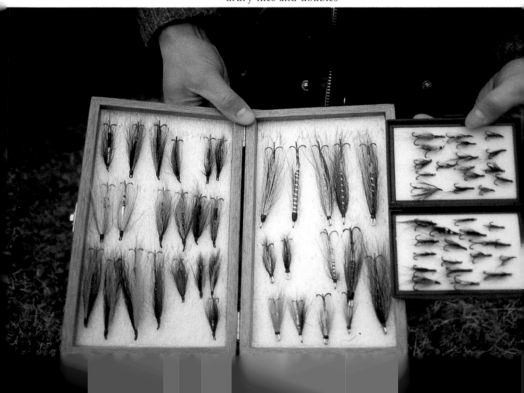

A three pound summer sea trout

Wading out to fish the Minister's Pool, Maxton, River Tweed

On the Tweed a
Scrogbank: cast
an autumn fly o
the tail of the
Birkie

On the
Juutuanjoki, nea
Lake Inari, Finn
Lapland – the
home of very
large trout

n Finnish Lapland:
large grayling makes a
iverside meal

Below left

the forest of
uttojoki, Finnish
apland: a three-pound
rown trout is
nhooked

Below right

sockeye in full
awning livery, taken
a trout rod, head of
ake Michalk, Alaska

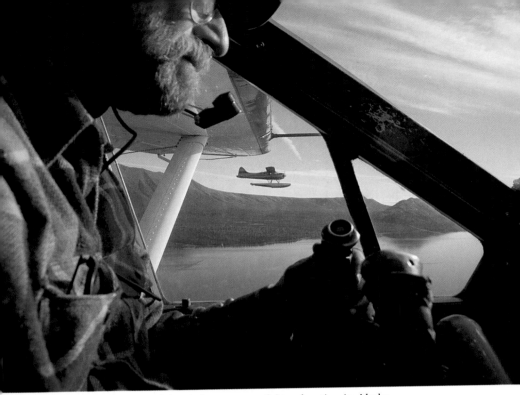

Flying in beavers to a fishing location in Alaska

Lake Michalk, Alaska

the fly away from the offer. It is far better not to know the rise has taken place and to react to the pull, which might be seconds later. If you do see fish – and it can be a marvellous experience to see the waters parting as a fish comes up to the fly – try to do absolutely nothing about it. Just wait. The seconds between the rise and the take are perhaps the longest known. Forty years after seeing my first fish take, I am still, sometimes, unreliable. It has helped to fish with a free reel however, and making it an absolute rule not to move any muscle until the reel speaks – that is until line is pulled off and the ratchet rasps, or screams. It usually gives a short burst of clicks, pauses and then pulls more. Some salmon will draw off five yards or more in the first pull. That can be spectacular. To interrupt the pull would be fatal. You might hook the fish, but it is more likely that you would not, or at best would hook the salmon forward in the mouth and only get a light hold.

It is easy to feel that you have missed a salmon, even after a large swirling rise when the reel fails to speak. You may already have called out 'Missed him!', with or without expletives when, suddenly, the reel goes and you are into him. Sometimes contact is only made seconds after the take, with or without a reel 'go', when you raise your rod. At times, you see nothing, but the line stops. There is a sensation of the sweep round being interrupted, as if a leaf or a twig had been touched in the stream. In these cases, let the line pull the fly in by continuing to come round in the flow. You will have to use your judgement, however. If you do nothing and there is no pressure on the hook to go in, as for example, in a gently flowing flat, you will have to help by raising the rod. Don't do it quickly. Lift it and, as it were, lean on the fish and bend the rod into it. Too strong a pull can be disastrous, either pulling the hook out or breaking in the fish if it happens at that point to be turning off downstream and making its first run.

It is extraordinary that a heavy, strong fish like a salmon can sometimes be so quiet in the take. I was fishing down the Irrigation pool on the Aboyne water of the Dee one evening recently when I began to get a succession of nudges. Just little touches, knocks or bumps, as if the pool had some very small trout in it and they were playing with the fly. I felt that these were salmon, however, but I was not sure how best to hook them. Then in a leaden glassy area of water beside the stream I distinctly felt nothing happening. You know what I mean. The fly seemed to have become lighter in some way. It had changed in its feel, not by being pulled, or nudged, or plucked, but by significantly feeling as if it had ceased to exist. I raised my rod and was into a fifteen pounder. It was extraordinary. The nudging, bumping and sucking takes must have been caused by the night, which was heavy and quiet and sultry.

Gentle takes like that, while quite often reported, are really untypical. Salmon usually let you know very clearly indeed that they have taken the fly, if you are just wise enough to leave them to do it. May takes are usually like this:

> bulge... (pause)... the line twitches and takes up the droop under
> the rod tip... (pause)... the line pulls and the reel speaks... and
> when it stops, or when you think it has pulled long enough, you
> raise the rod and are firmly into the fish.

The time for this whole sequence might be two seconds for a short, really fast take – the unusual kind – and up to ten seconds for the longest, slowest takes. Let me stick my neck out and say that the average is possibly four seconds on glides and slow streams. The slowest takes of all are by big fish to big flies on a sunk line in slow water. I would be surprised to find many people fishing with this tackle in May. In all this scenario of the take, of course, it is a blessing that much of it may take place before you are aware of it. I am certain that many first salmon are safely hooked, for example, without the fisher knowing much about it, except that the line finally goes tight, or 'gets stuck on the bottom', then moves.

The classic taking sequence, especially the pull and the taking of line, is the one we dream about and the one we remember. For many of us, it is the ultimate significant event in our fishing, the existential moment, which justifies the days of preparation and the hours of casting and it crowns the emotion of salmon fishing. I recall Grey's words, already quoted in the first chapter of this book:

> ...the supreme moment is undoubtedly the actual hooking of the
> fish... a shock of surprise and delight... a sense of complete
> achievement and satisfaction... (which) remains undiminished as
> years go on.

Sometimes the take is such an emotional high point that the fight which follows can seem slightly dull. In fact, fights with May springers seldom lack lustre. The salmon are fresh, many with sea lice still on their flanks. Some of the fish are large, and, in contrast to some of the large fish of autumn, they are large and vigorous. May in my mind is a time for long runs with heavy fish running downstream, crossing to the far bank, drowning the line and running hard up the distant side of the stream and leaping. The floating line helps you not to be broken when a heavy fish does this, because it drowns less than the intermediate or the neutral, but it is extremely difficult if a salmon has run downstream deeply and has then turned at speed and leapt on the other side of a stream to avoid alarming pressures on the hook hold and cast. You may think that our regular twelve-pound breaking strain leaders are coarse – too heavy for the size eight or ten flies we fish, but one or two experiences of fish drowning the line will change your mind. Equally, you may want sometimes to use a single-handed rod, say an eleven-footer to fish the smaller flies delicately. I have done this time and again myself. But the long rod is masterful at raising the line out of the drowning stream during the fight and that alone would recommend it for the spring on the Dee. In fact the spey casting we delight in on the Dee, often necessary because of difficult banks behind us, absolutely demands a rod such as the fifteen-foot carbon. Shorter rods are perfectly competent for playing salmon in open water, but add difficulties in casting, fly presentation (effective mending) and fish management during the fight. If you have a touch of the *kami kazi* angler in you, by all means indulge it and use a single-handed rod, but expect some difficult times and some losses which might have been avoided.

The flies we use in May on the Dee are the most satisfying salmon flies of the whole season. Now there's a subjective statement! As you would expect, behind such a statement lie decades of conditioning, of longing to catch Dee springers, of linking the slim, hair wing sixes and eights and tens with moments of unalloyed pleasure. Well, let me air my prejudices and describe the flies I like best. They are hairwings, usually Partridge long-shank trebles or small doubles, tied with gentle, flexible hair, black alone, black topped with orange or yellow, or mixed black, yellow and orange hair like a Willie Gunn. The bodies are good when they are black too, ribbed with gold wire, but I have, in recent seasons, become an addict of sinuous black hair over silver or gold flat tinsel. A fine trailing yellow hair tail can help. The fly should always have a streamlined, tapered look in the water, with a responsive tail or trailing wing which can wiggle. The stream sculpts the hair wing and tail into what I think of in its smaller sizes as a kind of nymph and in the larger sizes a little swimming eel. I like the hair to have its natural tapered ends and to date I have found no way of shortening hair without damaging this. I have used my thumb nail to 'layer' the hair at times, but the danger in this is that too much pressure can cause the fine fibres to curl. I abhor scissor-trimmed wings.

When I was in Alaska recently I sat down in the fishing lodge and tied up a range of hair wing salmon flies on single hooks (which worked well) and for some reason I moved away for a minute from the table, leaving a fly tied but in the vice. I was conscious of an American angler looking closely at it. It was a very pleasing dressing, tied with some long white and claret mixed hair, just what the Silvers of the Togiak would want the next day. The wing tapered beautifully and trailed out behind the size two Wilson hook I had used. I came back to varnish the head, and found my lovely tapered, trailing wing cut off

square above the bend of the hook. It was the result of the close
attention of – what shall I call him – a Bostonian admirer. He thought
he was helping by tidying up my trailing hair. I complained bitterly and
said no hair should ever be cropped on a wing like that. He said he
thought no hair should ever trail out behind the hook like that. We
were each heretics in the other's eyes. What was worse, he was unre-
pentant. I suppose benighted fishers like him keep their pyjamas in
drawers marked 'Pyjamas'.

I love the hair to taper and trail out behind the hook, whether it be a
single a double or a treble. I insist on it! I like a horizontal fly, lying in
the water with its trailing few hairs weaving and fluttering in the
current. My prejudice says that sparse, trailing, tapered hair is deadly,
and my prejudice keeps being reinforced by the salmon of the Dee in
May.

I must confess, however, to having become difficult to please in the
selection of a fly. Indeed, I may have become slightly too particular
about it. I have so often opened my fly box(es) on the river bank and
have looked at the scores of flies, indeed the hundreds of flies, in them
and have searched in vain for the one I want to tie on. So I have started
taking a basic fly-tying box to the waterside with me and, without a
vice, tying up the precise fly I want to fish. It is nearly always a dressed
treble, but I have also tied up a number of successful doubles in recent
years for the Dee in May. These flies are usually as I describe above,
basically black Squirrel hair or something responsive over a simple
body, plain colour, wire or tinsel. Bucktail is too stiff for small, active
flies. If you have a black Labrador, by the way, you may find, as I have,
that the best hair comes from the feathering under the tail. Of course,
you may have a formula involving a spaniel. Stoat's tail is brilliant, but,
alas, is often too short. Good, flexible black hair, tied on sparsely for
the Dee, looks magnificent over a silver body. Add a strand or two of
yellow, say dyed squirrel, and you have the perfect creation. It is not
just that these hand-tied flies work; it is that before they pleased the
salmon, they pleased me. Feeling good about the fly is important, but
feeling good about a fly you have just tied up is particularly rewarding
and when the salmon take it the satisfaction is enhanced. It is as if a
special harmony had been achieved.

The practice of tying up flies there and then is slightly precious, even
eccentric. I tie without a vice and use a very simple kit of black tying
silk, wire or tinsel and hair. Cobbler's wax drawn on to the tying silk
prepares it. I leave heads unvarnished for immediate use but I would
varnish them if I had time. You might think that the process is time
consuming. It is, but I would not do it if it did not add to the intense
pleasure of fishing. Choice of fly is central to my own fishing and I love
creating the fly for the day. It does mean, of course, that I have boxes

full of shop flies which I shall probably never fish again. That is a small price to pay for the delight of it all. In a week in May, just before writing this chapter, I had eleven Dee salmon on my own little trailing-tail flies, tens and eights. Nothing could be more satisfying. To gild the lily, several of the fish took like trout adding the pleasure of sight to the surprise of the draw.

On the Dee in May we fish late into the evening, indeed, we fish into the dusk, often taking the first dusk sea trout of the year in early May at Aboyne as we fish the late evening for salmon. Like most fish, salmon change their behaviour as the light goes. They move into shallower water and to some extent, they rove like sea trout and take up positions in the tails of the pools as well as in the streams and margins. They do not like clear evenings. On much of the the Aboyne water, there is a problem with the setting sun, which shines right down some of our best west–to–east pools like Jetty, Irrigation and the Lummels. The red light of the sunset appears to make the surface of the water brazen and interferes with the salmon's vision. It interferes with ours too if we look into the sunset upstream. Now, sunset fishing in west coast rivers is quite different. There, the dying light, although very red, comes from the tail and does not put fish off. I have had salmon and sea trout in these conditions on the Shiel and elsewhere. On the Dee, we like a high sky, slightly filmed over with cloud like a ground glass screen. Under such skies, the salmon come on to the take early, possibly by nine o'clock on a May evening and the taking time lasts until half-past-ten or even later. The salmon do go off in the deep dusk, although our diaries are full of fish which have taken unexpectedly in the dark when sea trout were being fished. It is probably just as well that salmon do call a halt, or body and soul might not hold together in May on the Dee. If you fish from nine in the morning until one, stop for lunch and try a cast or two on the streams in the afternoon, then return to fish after dinner, you can put in more hours than most of us have the strength to handle. Four or five days of this and exhaustion can set in. The youngest fishers, and the hungriest, or most frustrated may well try before breakfast. I've done that. I've seen the dawn come up on the Dee and it can be magnificent to be out at that time. But I now believe that fishing from nine to about three and putting in two hours in the evening is perfect, and it is often the evening casts which lead to the best takes.

Without diminishing in any way the delights of fly fishing at other times of the year, May holds a very high place in my affections as a salmon fisher. On middle Dee, May brings in the bulk of the spring fish. They come quickly up from the estuary – all the more so since the Dee proprietors bought off the estuary and coastal nets with the generous help of the Atlantic Salmon Conservation Trust. May fish come into a river still moderately high with water from the melting snows of the Cairngorms. The spring weather during the month usually settles and can often produce, from the first full week of May on, a benign, warm spell, worthy of anything the pastoral poets might have written about May mornings and shepherds with oaten flutes. The banks bloom, the trees burst into leaf. Summer is coming, but that is not the best news. The news we want to hear is that May has yet again brought the biggest run of the spring into the streams and pools of middle and upper river. May on Dee is a generous month. It allows us to practise the best of all the forms of salmon fishing I know – fishing a small fly on a floating line over clear streams and pools in a landscape of outstanding beauty and delight.

CHAPTER
7

Exporting the Dee

W<small>HEN</small> <small>SALMON</small> <small>FLY</small> <small>FISHERS</small> <small>ARE</small> <small>BEING</small> <small>HONEST</small>, which is almost all the time, they would admit, I think, that they are not really very scientific about fly selection. In my case this non-objectivity arises in the well-known form of the wish being father to the thought. Put in another way, it is the Dee which often biases me. That memorable and lovely river dwells in my mind. I think of it especially in May, and I remember the small flies and the feelings of fishing them over clear water lies. When I find myself fishing another river I often 'think Dee', because I want other rivers to be like that. Deep down I want my salmon, in the way I have described elsewhere in this book, to turn themselves into trout and move in a visual and often spectacular way to small flies swum over them. I want to export the techniques of the Dee as if it were the Ur-river. I wish it were. I could then also export all the delights of fishing that limpid, streamy water and solve the problems of fly size and type at one blow. You will not be surprised to find that it does not always work. In a salutary way, I am often reminded that there is no absolute template for salmon behaviour.

You do not necessarily need to travel very far to rediscover other patterns. The Tay fish, for example, usually demand a slightly larger fly. In summer conditions on the Tay, which may look as clear as the Dee and would make me want to fish size eight or ten, I have often found that the salmon prefer a six. In May and June I have sometimes found the small one-inch waddington, dressed with black and a mix of orange hair, to be the best on the Tay. In July a size six Shrimp has scored. In August and September the story is similar, where my Dee approaches would dictate a wisp of a fly, the Tay asks for a little more substance, more dressing, a trailing tail or even a small waddington. I have explained this to myself sometimes in terms of water clarity.

The Tay is often not so shiningly clear as the Dee. Then I bring myself
up short with the fact that in a river like the summer Helmsdale, which
even at its clearest is the colour of sherry, fish will sometimes only
come to a ten or a twelve. There is also the question of depth of salmon
lie. The Dee, typically, holds its salmon in two- to five-foot lies. The
Tay has both a less streamy character than the Dee and greater volume
and typically offers salmon more depth.

If the variations, river to river, were only in the order of a couple of
hook sizes, that would perhaps be containable. From time to time,
however, I fish waters where the taking size may be so grossly different
that I begin to look for special reasons. Interestingly, I also remember
traditions on the Dee itself which hint that my addiction to small flies
in summer may in fact only be one mode of tackling salmon and, much
as I would like to dragoon all salmon into that mode to suit my tastes,
it is my own thinking which has to be broadened.

In the summer of 1991 I was introduced to the glorious waters of
the middle Namsen in Norway. In many ways, this superb river is the
Scottish Dee writ large. Its lower reaches sweep through glides and
long pools like larger versions of the beats of the lower Dee. The
middle waters of the Namsen near Grong have a wilder character; they
pour over shingle and boulders, furl round massive rocks, pit and wave
in long, fast, holding streams over innumerable salmon lies and, in
places, form dark, deep pools in gorges where the trees cling to fissured
rocks rising sheer from the river. The faster waters of the Namsen seem
to have been born from the same act of creation as the Dee. Both pour
over pre-Cambrian rock, glittering with mica and felspar. The clarity of
the water is there, the rushing, streamy lies, the long vee-like tails to
the pools. Yet the size of the Namsen brings all these similarities into
doubt. It is the Dee magnified. That proposition, however, has another
side. The Dee enlarged is the fisher diminished – cut down to size.
I have felt this before on the Tana in northern Norway, and on some
Canadian and Alaskan rivers. You have only to wade into the edge of a
Namsen stream to feel both exhilarated and threatened by its force, or
to look down from the long boat through ten or twelve feet of powerful, ultra-clear water, to realise that the Namsen restores awe to the
fishing experience in the way a tiger might to those who have grown
used to cats.

The Namsen salmon also have the quality of big game. The lodge at
Holandsay was filled with casts of forty-pounders. My host there, Nat
Reed, had tales to tell of reels emptied of backing, of marathon pursuits
downstream by boat following great fish hooked on the fly. Everything, it seemed, enjoyed a shift of dimension; it was on a bigger scale.

On a clear, fast moving stream in the Dee in summer, you would
think of size eight or ten, perhaps even twelve, wispy trebles or little

doubles, and you would fish these flies high in the water with a floating line or a neutral. The image which possesses me, as I have said elsewhere, is that of turning salmon into trout. Finding a river with many of the characteristics of the Dee, it was entirely predictable that, large as the river was, I expected the Atlantic salmon of the Namsen to behave like the same species in the Dee. In past years, some anglers have found that they did. For me on that first visit, they did not. Fishing different sizes of my Golden Stoat with its trailing tails, I had no more than one pluck to a size eight Drury in a rippled glide under a bright sun. The first fish to come in that week were grilse, very small fresh fish, three or four pounds in weight, tiddlers, a kindergarten of salmon on a river famous for its enormous, kyped fish. Yet even these *kinder* wanted long, light tubes. The local wisdom was to fish a polythene tube with a two-and-a-half- or three-inch Brook's Sunrise Shadow – black goat's hair, long and flexible with three or four long strands of peacock herl tied in as the trailing surprise, a fly developed on the Laerdal, and it was this two-and-a-half-inch fly which took the first salmon of the week.

There were other Namsen creations too. One boatman successfully urged me to fish his long, light, braided silver tube with a fronded end to the body, a thick but very flexible black hair wing of some five inches in length which had mixed in with its dark fibres, several thin streams of wire braid and a cluster of green fibres, plastic I thought. This he explained to me was a herring in the water. I didn't laugh. I tried it out and raised a salmon twice to it in a way which reminded me of how salmon behave when a prawn is swum disturbingly over them. The fish boiled very fast at the fly in the margin of a stream. I left the fly swimming in the hope the fish would come again and take it. He didn't; it was the next cast before he moved again. This time the fish leapt from the water and descended on the herring-fly. In both cases the fish did not take the the fly so much as attack it.

Thinking about large flies, I naturally think of spring and autumn in Scotland. At these times, large flies are fished in cold and usually high water and the preference for the two-inch fly well sunk is neatly rationalised as triggering off some kind of sea feeding reaction in salmon in waters similar in temperature to those of the Atlantic. But there are other stories to be told about the success of larger flies on the Dee and Spey and elsewhere when waters are not cold. Among these you will find the family of flies known as 'Toshes'.

My concept of a Tosh is that it is a tube fly, long, often two inches or more, tied with trailing hair, usually including yellow. 'Tosh' on Deeside and Speyside is a generic name, used like a broad sweep of the hand. I have asked once or twice what the name means and the nearest I have come to an answer is that there was a keeper with a dog called Tosh whose yellow hair created these flies. I did not have the pleasure of meeting 'Tosh', but my friend Gordon McBain did and his Purple McBain is often called the Purple Tosh, or McBain's Tosh and is a remarkable fly. Gordon McBain fishes this fly in all manner of sizes and styles, but the original form of the fly was dressed on a long, light polythene tube and one of the most successful sizes is two-and-three-quarter inches long – a light flexible, sinuous, hairy creation which swims like a little eel and which is a first-class killer of fish in the Dee from the opening day right through the season. I saw the McBain doing tremendous execution one May evening on the Dee and had a dozen of these long tubes tied up in Aberdeen. The following opening day on the Dee, February first, with water temperatures hovering just above freezing, after failing to take anything on my waddingtons, I fished a light McBain nearly three inches long and took a springer. That was the beginning of my deep respect for the long, light fly. Over several seasons I built up experience of the Purple McBain working. It has taken fish in cold and warmer water and indeed, in the hands of Gordon McBain himself has held its own in Highland waters against all comers, including the remarkable Ally's Shrimp with its long trailing orange tail.

Toshes, like the McBain, have close relatives. The very long ultra-flexible Collie Dog can present the fish with six or seven inches of lure when the curly dog hair straightens out in the water. That pattern is surely the eel fly *par excellence*. On a tube, the Collie Dog is sometimes dressed only as a long, fine tress of hair attached to a bare polythene or aluminium tube. In the water the fly may in fact swim apparently well away from its hooks. Original versions of this fly, which I have seen in Brora, attached the long hair to the neck of a single hook. Fish seemed to have no difficulty in getting the hook, proving that salmon do not necessarily take a long fly from behind. On the Namsen, one of the grilse I caught on a long Brook's Sunrise Shadow was hooked on the outside of the angle of the jaw. The fish had clearly taken the big tube across its length, perhaps even attempting to take the long fly from the head as a fish or an eel might be taken in the sea.

Fishing the Namsen has jolted my memory of long flies on the Dee and elsewhere. It has also reminded me that summer fish sometimes become resistant to the subtle small fly presented in a delicate way. I have seen pools on the Dee filled with grilse which would not even move to inspect the small flies I swam over them, but which, suddenly seeing a long tube, boiled at it and took it well. I have also seen fresh summer grilse on the Naver which spurned all mended and slowly presented small flies, turn in pairs or better and pursue a long light fly moved fast over their pool.

On the Namsen, fish often take the long tube when it is being hand-lined back to the boat. I had an interesting experience in the middle of a very un-dark July night, fishing a large deep pool in which I had seen a salmon move. The pool, Olla's House, has a fine wide streamy head with a great force of water which collects under a cliffy, fissured left bank and scours a deep channel in front of a series of long hog-backed rocks. This stream deepens to form a great, green eddying hole flanked on the right bank by a wide, gliding stream some eight to ten feet deep. I was wading the edge of this glide, deep enough to wet my elbows, when I saw a salmon move in the stream over the deep hole on what seemed to be the far side. I asked the boatman to take me over and let me try the lie from the ridge of rocks on the far side. When I got there, the stream looked different, more turbulent, less fishy, dark green, deep and frightening. As often happens when you cross a river, the lie seems to change completely. That one was not just off the rocks at all, where the depth was. It was somewhere on the outer apron of the stream, a long cast away and not easy to fish because the turbulent rush pulled the fly off the likely water between the deep stream and the glide.

The obvious thing to do was to boat the lie from the other side, where I had originally been wading, and, with the boat held on the oars, I covered the likely water with the long Sunrise tube fished on a neutral line. On the second or third cast while I was handlining the long line back from the dangle, I had a take and after some excitement landed a strong fish around fifteen pounds, a Namsen tiddler perhaps, but I was not complaining. Fishing down through the rest of the lie, after another couple of casts I thought my Sunrise might have hanked back on the cast and, swinging the line back to the boat from the rod top, I caught the loop in my hands and quickly stripped it in to inspect the fly. As the Sunrise was streaking in towards me a salmon followed it and boiled hard at the speeding fly. That was a large fish. It did not touch the fly, perhaps mercifully, because I was there, caught in a most unprofessional pose, handlining the fly in for inspection with all manner of coils of line in the boat and in the water beside.

What would have happened if the big fish which sloshed at the hand-lined, stripped fly had in fact taken hold? I have often thought about that in a kind of hair-raising, fantasy way – hooking a salmon on a hand line. It would be immediately and directly felt, not interpreted through the rod with the usual signals – the droop of line going, the pull, the reel speaking, then the rod bending into the weight of the fish. On a short handline it would be raw, immediate contact with a muscular and potentially violent fish. Yes, what indeed would happen next? Would the line suddenly tighten and go in a draw? And for that matter, what does a salmon draw feel like when you are operating a short handline? Perhaps the fish would pulse, then run, taking line through my hand. Would it burn my fingers, or would I drop the line and frantically take up slack once I was sure the hooks were in? Alas, I do not know, for, except in dreams, it has never happened to me. It *nearly* happened to me on the Namsen with a fish which could have been a monster. I learned afterwards from Nat Reed's fascinating Namsen diaries that Olla's House, where this happened, is a pool famous for its enormous salmon. In the opinion of the boatman, I had possibly moved one of these.

You might wonder what I did next. The adrenalin was certainly flowing. I cast out at once and, stripping the line in to give the fish as fast a presentation of the fly as possible, I had another pursuit. A fish arched through the stream at the Brook's Sunrise, but again did not touch it. The fast, long tube was bringing the fish up, but while the first fish took strongly and well, and engulfed the fly, the others seemed merely to be disturbed by it. I had, of course, recently played and landed a fish in that water and that may be a material fact. The fish I did take was so well hooked that the fly had to be taken out through the gills.

Talking to the other rods about this question of fish apparently shunning traditional approaches and taking large light flies moved quickly, one friend, Bo Ivanovic, an experienced and successful fly fisher, said that on the Namsen, he always left his fly trailing in the water when the boat was motoring back upstream and he had had grilse take it at what must be several upstream knots per hour. When you add the speed of the stream to the upstream way of the boat, the speed of a fly fished like that is very high indeed.

In Norway, the long, light tube fly seems to have a huge following. The Alta flies I have seen have been of this kind, two-and-a-half or three inches long, black hair-wing tubes with cheeks or bright fibres dressed in. It might be argued that most of the fish taking these long flies were very fresh into the river, when fish are bolder and less discriminating than they might be a week later. There is something in this argument, but I have seen fish in Scotland which would not rise to smaller flies and which were showing all the signs of becoming stale, rising immediately to a sinuous, lissom, Collie Dog or an Ally's Shrimp with its inch-and-a-half trailing tail. There is also a school of thought in Norway that holds that the larger fly is necessary for the larger fish. This is hard to substantiate. If the local style is to fish long tubes, the boatmen will put pressure on you to try them. If long flies are on regularly, they will almost certainly take fish regularly. Also, on rivers where there is a tendency to harl from boats, or to cast from boats held against the current, it may be that long tubes are thought to have a more attractive presence in the streams. Rivers like the Namsen, Alta and Tana, have deep lies. Fish have to be raised to follow and take a fly. I can well understand how the Dee with its three or four foot deep lies would have a different optical problem for salmon. Deeper rivers might also have a kind of inertia problem too. Large salmon might need a big stimulus to make them want to pursue a fly swum several feet above them. I am not, however, going to be drawn to the conclusion that large flies are necessary to take large fish.

In a sense, therefore, being shaped by the Dee implies more than just being in love with small flies fished on a floating line. The Dee tradition embraces something of long, sinuous pursuit flies also. Exporting the tradition of the Dee is therefore less restricted than I implied earlier. Inside the Dee experience are the longer flies which salmon fishers have found to be highly successful elsewhere. There are two modes of salmon fly fishing, as it were a nymph one and an eel one. Richard Waddington was one of the fly fishers who expounded this well in his books on the 'elverine' design of fly which now bears his name. My wanting particularly to export the small spring and summer flies of the Dee is perhaps just my deep longing for the idyll of May mornings at Aboyne. The Namsen has its idylls too, and its sagas. A visit to that glorious river has gone a long way to curing me of being too selective. It is good to remember in all our fishing that it is unlikely that the behaviour of a creature as vigorous and complex as the salmon can be enshrined in a single proposition.

CHAPTER
8

Open to the north-west

FISHING WATERS always have an elemental link with the rocks and soil they lie over and through this we can, in an almost poetic way, reach back and touch the act of creation. Put in more practical terms, anglers are usually very conscious of the shapes of the glens and valleys they fish in and they feel as a present reality the ancient scouring of glaciers or the inundation by the sea which shaped them. They wade over old rocks as smooth as iron plating and newer rocks with ledges to trap the unwary wader. They walk over peat moors to hill lochs and follow burns down to shingly rivers; they drift the many shapes of bays on small and large lochs and all this rich contact with the very bones of the earth illuminates the fishing. Angling landscapes are read like special kinds of text in an arcane language which fishers learn to interpret and translate into tactics.

In the West Highlands of Scotland we have a whole series of sea trout waters in glens shaped by the lie of the bedrock and the ice to produce substantial valleys with a north-west to south-east trend. These glens hold waters which have gained a reputation as the best sea trout fishings in Scotland. I am thinking as I write of Maree, Shiel, Stack, Hope and others. These evocative waters share many features. The ideal pattern seems to be that of a large loch in a north-west facing glen, linked by a short river with good flow to a sandy sea loch. The shape and aspects of these waters, however, are not always what dominates a fishing day there. You are conscious of another elemental force, the wind. These waters are open to the north west and it is from this airt that the wind comes for drifting and dapping or searching out the waves with a team of big wet flies. The drifts are often long, and the open reaches produce waves, streaked with foam, brown water lapping over shingles and rocks on the shore and deepening into bays with rushy and wooded hills rising steeply from the edge. On these drifts you will see many examples of the west wind working on water – the steady wave with the ripples within it as a kind of secondary feature, the glassy slicks among the rough water, the foam roads and, as the wind becomes unsteady and puffs up and down, we see the wandering dark patches of scud. These lochs are atmospheric places, where the wind above and the rocks below shape waters of the highest order in sea trout fishing.

The wind on a loch determines not only how the ripple and waves affect the drifts on a given day, or even a given hour. In the longer term, the wind and the wave mould the characteristics of the bays. In shallow water they sculpt the bed of the loch. They sift and deploy the gravel. Where waves lap peaty banks they gouge out curious pockets and lies, sometimes revealing ancient tree stumps long lost in the peat. Where boulders lie on the bed, perhaps strewn there by the ancient ice sheets, wind and wave create what are virtually streams in still water where fish may lie as if waiting for food in a river.

Fishing these larger sea trout lochs is almost always done by boat, even if I can recall some days and many evenings, when wading the loch was successful. You can take brown trout and finnock wading and casting a fly from the bank during the day, but sea trout, when the sun is up are usually found in water deeper than you would normally reach by wading and casting. They are beyond the typical trout and salmon depths. Typically, a fifteen- to twenty-foot deep drift is good for sea trout, but for brown trout the best water is under ten feet and for salmon under six. Sea trout may come close inshore in the dusk and dark, but that is a different game.

Drifting down a long beat on Maree, for example, can be like reading a text whose meaning is pieced together from clues. You might drift, for long periods, parallel to a straight shore, holding the right depths in this way. Where a burn flows in it might lay a ridge of gravel out into the loch and even if you were not able to see the changing depths this would cause, the fish activity would tell you. You might suddenly find brown trout plucking at the wet flies or cavorting over the dap. As the water shallows over the gravel, you might raise a salmon. Sometimes the salmon is the shallowest taker of all, coming to your flies in only three feet of water. The long, steady drift for sea trout well off the bank may also suddenly be punctuated by trout and a chance movement of a salmon, revealing the presence of an underwater ridge or island. In sea trout fishing, knowing the depths and shape of the loch bottom is absolutely vital. It is as though we fish with all our sense alert, gauging the wind, seeing the story on the surface of the loch and responding to all these signals. A sixth sense, however, working like an echo sounder, comes partly from knowledge and partly from intuition, making you aware of the unseen loch bed and often that is the key to the best fishing for sea trout.

The late summer day you are fishing a north-west loch may well have quite clearly marked phases entirely dictated by the wind. On Maree I have often seen the day begin with a tiny ripple, raised by a wind with hardly enough power to puff out the dapping line. At lunch time, we have pulled ashore in complete calm, and have eaten our picnic as we gazed at a still loch with all the hills reflected in it. But by the end of the break the day wind has sprung up from the west and has stiffened during the afternoon and both dap and wet fly has worked well. That wind is usually a thermal one, drawn off the cooler sea as the day heats up the air over the land. These afternoon breezes are typical of the coast and they may not penetrate far inland. This is where the large north-west sea lochs benefit. They lie close to the sea, and more importantly, they lie open to its day winds.

What in fact does the wind do to make sea trout take well during the day? River fishers know the sea trout as a very shy fish except for a short period of idiocy when the fish are running fresh from the sea. It is not surprising that the main fishing for sea trout in rivers takes place at night when an approach is possible. Sea trout in still lochs are very difficult fish indeed, although I have sometimes done well by fishing a dry fly and a long line, letting it sit out for a while, then occasionally dragging it a few inches. Calm water makes fish go deep because they feel insecure. Ripple corrugates the roof over their heads and a good wave seems to bring them up from the deeper water and be 'on the fin', almost in a hunting mood not far below the surface of the holding drifts. I do not really know why I say 'almost' in a hunting mood because sea trout following a rolling and dancing dap are unambiguously going for it, leaping at it, splashing at it in what is often a very vigorous way. We say that river sea trout are nocturnal feeders. But are they in fact, or are they merely night takers because their guard is down? The main fishing for sea trout on lochs is undoubtedly by day and in my view that is simply because the wind allays their fears. Sea trout feed by day when they are in salt water. We often see them veeing in and out of seaweed. Why should they become purely nocturnal when in the river, except through caution? I have explored sea trout fishing at night on lochs and several times I have found it to be good, but not in the drifts we follow by day. At night the fish come further inshore and may even be found right in with their noses on the shingle, especially near burns.

Dapping is a very popular form of fly fishing these large sea trout lochs and many anglers think of their success in this as one of getting the right wind for the dap. It is certainly true that without the right wind, the dapping floss will not blow out into that great arc in front of the boat and the large dapping fly will not float and dance and roll as it should. But the wind is far more important than that. Dapping is not only an art of the rod, the wind and the waves. It is also an art of concealment and the way the wave conceals the fisher is critical to its success. In a light breeze not only will the dap work poorly; it will not bring up the fish well, quite simply because the fish is wary of moving up to a calm surface. In a good breeze, the dap not only does not scare the fish but it excites them inordinately by the way it moves on and in the surface. The fly vees and trails up the sides of waves with a wet look. It bounces and daps. Sometimes it just seems to fly, hardly touching the water at all. It is unforgettable to see substantial sea trout leaping vigorously from the loch to follow a low-flying dap.

Dapping, much more than wet fly fishing, is a visual business, but it is no easier to fish a dapped fly because of this. Indeed, many of the rises we see to the dap are misses. The sea trout are stimulated to rise to the fly with vigorous swirls, or splash or leap out of the water over the fly not unlike the way a brown trout in a loch will sometimes arc out over the dropper fly and take it either on the way down, or immediately after crashing back into the water. I see this as a kind of drowning rise, bringing the too-mobile surface fly into the water where, in its own element, the fish can take the fly well. It is interesting to reflect that a dapping fly is virtually out of the angler's control when the wind is at its best. We can, of course, alter the angle of the rod, swing it a bit to the side this way and that or shorten line. We can add a lead shot to ballast the floss and by knotting the floss, or shortening it, in some way try to improve our control over the fly. But, apart from these rather crude forms of control, a dapping fly is fished by the wind and the wind, as the book says, 'Bloweth where it listeth'. This lack of control has two effects. On the one hand the random dancing fly raises sea trout from greater depths and in a more excited way than any wet fly does. On the other, the rises we provoke lead to more misses than in any other form of fishing. Often we are spectators as much as fishers in this. Wet fly is a far more efficient way of hooking sea trout, but on most days it does not produce a fraction of the surface activity which comes to the dap. I treasure one or two rare days when my wet fly has absolutely wiped the eye of the dap, but in fact they seldom happen. Fished in the same boat as a dap, wet fly may be the ideal complement, however. The dap raises the fish, but misses it (or the fish misses the fly); the wet fly catches the attention of the aroused fish, which takes the more controlled, sub-surface wet fly and is hooked.

Salmon will sometimes take the dap too. I have seen this happen fairly regularly, but I am often aware when a salmon is hooked, that the fly has been actually in the water or, when the salmon has risen to the surface fly and has missed it, I am conscious of the fish wanting the fly to be in or under the surface rather than on it. On more than one occasion, I have seen salmon come to a dap with an extended small

treble hook below it. That hook is certainly in the water and the rise
form has convinced me that the salmon has in fact taken the treble
rather than engulfing the whole fly in the way a sea trout would. There
is no doubt that salmon are brought up by the dap. They come up and
follow; they swirl; they may turn away and show back and fin as they
do so. I have never seen a salmon arch over a dap in the way a sea trout
does. More often, if a salmon is raised by the dap, it will swirl at it, or
vee the surface beside it, then turn and take a wet fly fished by another
rod in the boat. This ties in with the general picture of salmon in
Scotland not being taken on a dry fly, even if they will unambiguously
come to a small fly fished so near the surface that it was within the
surface film, but on the underside.

There are tantalising reaches on many of our sea trout lochs with
names like 'salmon rock', 'salmon point', 'salmon bank' and the like.
On some days I have decided to concentrate on taking a salmon rather
than a sea trout. I have, as it were, changed into a salmon gear. I have
fished the same rod – my wet fly eleven-footer or in the older days my
cane nine-foot-six or ten-footer and I have set out for the specific places
where salmon lie and show in the beat. Changing mental gear to fish
salmon has interesting phases. It involves talking salmon to the boatman on the way out. Boatmen will often recall seeing fish moving,
raising them to the dap. They may also talk pointedly about misguided
rods who spurned sea trout for a morning to try for a salmon and the
more frank may imply that your are soft in the head to consider it,
because the salmon is not half as interesting as a sea trout to fish for.
The best of the boatmen, however, will know that to drift slowly in on
a shallow reef or a sunk rock or the underwater ridge out from a headland is a rather subtle art. Often this means holding the boat off the lie
and positioning it well. The whole process, for boat and rod, is a kind
of slowing down, almost a dulling of the senses, reflecting the fact that
the salmon is a much more deliberate fish than even the largest sea
trout.

I usually fish a floating line for loch salmon, although in recent years,
I have found the neutral line to be excellent. It just sits within the
surface, but it allows the fly to fish a few inches down. Salmon do not
like to break the surface as they take. They head and tail, of course, and
show a fin and a tail, but the best and most sincere takes are usually
those which pull the line and then show a boil on the top, indicating
that the fish has taken the fly deliberately and slowly and will, in most
cases, have hooked itself well.

I have spoken of big sea trout wet flies, and on many windy north-
west lochs the best sea trout flies are heavily dressed sixes. When I say
'big' I mean big in the dressing also. I love double- or treble-hackled
Zulus, flies like Kate McLaren with brown hackles tied over bushy

black ones. Soldier Palmers ribbed with ginger hackles right down the shanks and Loch Ordies with their brown and pale hackles bushing over the body. Sometimes, in good winds, I have fished dapping flies on the bob of my two-fly wet cast. I have had experimental wadding-tons ties in Black Pennell style fishing a huge rolling dap over a small treble. I have had Dark Mackerels tied on long-shank sixes and on one-inch waddington shanks and these flies have worked for sea trout. For salmon in lochs, it is always necessary to go down in size of fly. It is also wise to change down in weight of dressing. I like a small drury-style of fly on the tail, say an eight or a ten dressed treble, unless the wave is high when a size larger may be tied on. On the bob, the fly position the salmon and the sea trout like best, I would fish a size eight Black Pennell, Zulu, Dark Mackerel, or similar, but not nearly so heavily dressed as for sea trout.

The approach, as I have said, is slow, the boat is held and the fly is fished with deliberate slow pulls of the line and it is brought close to the boat with the rod at a high angle to give a good working of the bob as the cast comes out. Good bob-fly fishing is highly skilled. It is a kind of writing on the surface of the wave or just under it. The right action gives that lovely wet look to the bob fly as it comes to the surface and makes a small dragging trail – into the loch, up to the surface, cutting the film, trailing. ...It is tremendous fishing! Sometimes I think I am in there with the fly. It is mesmeric. And when the salmon moves, it is, if you are lucky, a pull which signals a take or a half glimpse of the fish as it follows and turns on the fly. I say a hidden pull is lucky, because it reduces the temptation to react to the salmon too quickly. I lost fish and missed fish and foul hooked fish in my early days at loch salmon fishing because I could not stay my hand. Perhaps I boast if I say I now can wait the two or three vital seconds after a fish seems to take until the fish has turned away with the fly. It is an amazing experience to prepare for the drift on the lie, steadily come in on the salmon, carefully work your cast through the water, then suddenly become aware of the fish moving to you. Every hormone, enzyme and whatever else the ductless glands pump into your blood, shouts to you to act. If you do, you will miss the offer. It is *par excellence* mind over body which brings success in a loch salmon take. There is, of course, the dreamy take, the surprise. You are looking at the hills and not paying much attention to the cast, which is, anyway, your unpteenth unproductive cast over the lie. Then you lift your rod and you find you are unexpectedly fast into a salmon. That kind of take loses something, of course, but it does solve the problem of hasty reaction. To slow myself down, I have at times, taken to saying things to delay action when I see a take. For example, I might say quite deliberately to my colleague in the boat, 'There he is!', making sure I do nothing with my rod until I have ended the sentence.

Most large sea trout lochs have runs of salmon into them. Some even have had, or may still have, spring fish in them. Maree certainly has May fish, but W.J.M. Menzies, that famous Chief Inspector of Salmon Fisheries for Scotland and salmon guru, before and after the Second World War held that lochs like Hope and Assynt and Stack had runs of fish in March which were never fished. As far as I know they are still unfished. I know that Loch Shiel runs April and May salmon into it, because we have seen them and caught them in the river below in these months and they do not stay in the pools there. The problem with early salmon coming into these north-west lochs is that they run in small numbers and are virtually lost in the large tracts of water involved. The May salmon I have taken in Maree have all been at the Kinlochewe end about mid-May. There are certainly much earlier fish, but few anglers tackle the loch as early as this. Indeed, the earliest salmon on many of these large lochs fall to trolling. I have, in my day, trolled lochs like Naver at Easter and have seen Hebridean lochs and West Highland lochs trolled as late as June on the way out to fly drifts. Some of the fish taken in this way are clearly salmon which have been in the lochs for some weeks. Trolling is dull fishing, especially if it is a question of motoring miles with a toby trailing out behind. In my early trolling days on Loch Naver it was much more intimate, rowing alone in the boat and trolling a sprat over likely water. In a way, I am glad that there are runs of fish into Highland lochs which we do not exploit. It is a form of conservation. Similarly, on great sea trout lochs salmon are neglected when the sea trout arrive. There is also the feature that sea trout lochs whose stocks are in decline, often seem to turn into salmon fisheries. I have in mind the case of Loch Stack which was a fine sea trout fishery in the 1960s and by the next decade was known as a salmon fishery with a few sea trout. This is partly selectivity on our part as fishers. When sea trout numbers are low, we may spend more time looking for salmon and fishing them. I hardly think it is competition for redds, or excessive feeding competition between sea trout and salmon parr. Yet, salmon do sometimes seem to fill a sea trout vacuum.

I am writing this chapter after two years in which our western sea trout in Scotland and Ireland have been in decline. The fish have not disappeared, but it is true to say that the stocks in some areas of the west have been badly depleted. It is important to try to keep some perspective in this current decline. In some localities it has been far less marked than others, for the very good reason that the sea trout is a local sea feeder, unlike the salmon which migrates long distances to ocean feeding grounds. For example, in 1990 when thirteen of the sixty-two Scottish fishery districts returned their lowest sea trout figures since 1952, four districts recorded their highest returns. There have been many years in the last century when sea trout figures have soared and others when they have sunk disastrously low. This should not make us sit back and let the fluctuations happen, assuming that all will come right in the end. I think it does no harm, however, to bring a longer perspective into the variations of a very local migratory fish. What is alarming about sea trout decline in recent years is that the pressure on inshore sea fishing has been very high and a number of freshwater fishery managers believe that the sea, rather than freshwater environment, holds the key to major stock fluctuations. For instance, scallop and prawn fishing grossly disturbs the sea bed. Sand eel fishing, for fish meal of all things, seriously affects the stocks of this vital sea trout food. There are many causes for anxiety and action groups in Scotland, Ireland and Wales are working to establish causes for the decline and to take steps to restore stocks where possible.

My perspective in writing about these marvellous West Highland lochs includes the lean years as well as the fat ones, covering over thirty seasons of fishing in them for sea trout. During that time there has been at least one major outbreak of disease. Some seasons have yielded more large fish than others. There have been good finnock years when masses of young fish have been tugging at the fly and other years when we have wondered where the young generation of sea trout were. Stocks of sea trout have weathered all these variations and have recovered, sometimes with great speed. I am, I must admit, more worried about the current decline that I have been about all the other variations except the decimation in the early 1970s by UDN disease. I am not wholly pessimistic about sea trout, however, even if I am disturbed by their recent decline. It would be wonderful if what I write here in the early 1990s were rapidly to go out of date and the stocks of sea trout would again rise to the sort of peaks we have enjoyed in the past. I write about the fish as I have known them in a lifetime of fishing in the West Highlands, celebrating them and the summer salmon which accompany them in these treasured waters – these evocative and beautiful short rivers and large lochs in high-sided glens open to the fishing winds from the west.

CHAPTER
9

North Sea river

THERE IS BOTH LOGIC AND A LIE in saying that the Tweed is three rivers. Gaul was said by Caesar to be divided into three parts and, had he been fortunate enough to stand on the banks of Tweed, as many Roman soldiers eventually did, he might have been tempted to divide the river into thirds. After all, there is a clear section from Kelso to the sea, and its top boundary is very well marked out by the great Junction pool at Kelso where Teviot joins Tweed. This lower section, with its slowing flow, turns through great haughs of fertile land in the Merse of Berwick, a wide, flat river with deep dubs, massive pools, and below Coldstream, has more and more of the smell of the sea about it before it reaches the tidal stretches and the North Sea itself at Berwick-upon-Tweed. Yes, that is a quite logical section of Tweed – if you stand far enough back from the water and if you really do not know it as an angler.

Perhaps I am blaming Caesar for a division he did not make. I have, I suppose, longed to get my own back on him for difficulties his Latin placed in my way in my schooldays. Yet, if he had drawn a line at Kelso to mark the upper limit of the fat and fertile Lower Tweed, he would have had little trouble in drawing a second at the head of Bole-side where the Ettrick joins the river bringing down wild hill water from the twin streams, Yarrow and Ettrick, speaking of a hinterland of high Border hills, lochs, heather and grouse. More than any other tributary, the Ettrick divides the Tweed. It is the great left turn for the spring fish and the natural stopping place for the earliest autumn salmon. Those of us who fish the Tweed above this point often feel like the forgotten people. Races of salmon which have never tasted upper Tweed waters run the Ettrick. It can be galling to wait for the upper runs to arrive, partly because Ettrick fish arrive first, but partly because

Ettrick and Yarrow can bring water down to the Tweed when the upper river starves in a rain shadow. There are upper Tweed anglers with meaner temperaments than I or my readers, who derive some satisfaction in autumn from the fact that Ettrick can overdo it, obliterating the middle and lower Tweed with muddy and peaty water when the upper Tweed remains clear. Teviot to Ettrick indeed marks out a very important section of the river. On middle Tweed lie many lovely, streamy, excellent holding beats, Floors, Rutherford, Mertoun and Maxton, Dryburgh, Bemersyde, Tweedswood, Pavilion, Boleside. The names are like a great peal of bells. This middle section of the river is glorious and its streams and rocky pools give us excellent, lively water in which some of the finest salmon fishing in Scotland is to be found.

Caesar's successors camped in the upper Tweed also, on what today are marvellous scenic sites on grassy hills, like the camp at Caddonlea, near Clovenfords, where a splendid section of wooded valley unrolls from Yair to Ashiestiel and Holylee. I wonder what that landscape looked like in the first century AD when Agricola and the Roman army arrived. Were the steep sides of Yair and Fairnilee impenetrable wet woodlands, saughs, red-berried elder, thorn, gorse, birch and a daunting tangle of brambles and wild rose? I list these, because in the years I lived on the hill above Clovenfords unkempt parts of the land and the river banks below grew these trees and shrubs in profusion. Perhaps in these early times there were also, as the findings in the bogs suggest, oak, chestnut, elm and pine, leaving only the tops of the hills bare. I do get the impression sometimes that the upper Tweed valley has not changed radically for a millenium. The upper river has always been a place with a special conceit of itself and it asserts a very individual landscape. The upper Tweed carries a sense of being moorland, and being different. Its waters are those of its source at Tweedsmuir, where like the Clyde, it drains grassy and heathery land and tends to run clear off this stony territory. It gains volume from the waters of the Lyne, the Manor and the Eddleston and takes on between Peebles and Innerleithen the character of a fine stream-and-pool salmon river. The Leithen and the Traquair waters swell it still further and through Caberston, Juniper Bank, Scrogbank, and Holylee the Tweed improves as a fishing water and forms many excellent salmon pools and runs. It yields some of its best fish on the tumbling water and 'weils' from Elibank and Thornilee down to Yair and Fairnilee. Upper Tweed is a salmon river *per se*, an autumn fishery for the most part, with good sea trout adding to the bags. It is also throughout its length a fine trout water, wilder than the trout fishing of the middle river, but memorable.

The truth is that the Tweed is *at least* three rivers. The lie is that, when you are an angler regularly fishing on Tweedside, it is in fact a profusion of waters – a lifetime and more of fishing in itself, and like

life itself, is always redefining familiar things and showing new
emphases. It is paradoxical to say that fishers like me who think they
know the water well, are always conscious of knowing little through
fact and much through speculation and intuition. I find it often a
generous river, yielding salmon predictably, as if angler and fish had
read the same books. Then I have periods when I find the river sly,
failing to show autumn fish when and where it should, running its fish
hard when the levels suggest that they should stop to become our
residents, and communicating dourness when all the indicators are for
spree. There are many times as an upper Tweed fisher when the river
gives me, particularly, a sense of being thrawn, coming from a high
moorland where the philosophy is one of dourness and resistance to
suggestion. In the middle Tweed I have felt, especially in autumn
floods, that the Tweed was a creature unreformed by history, primitive,
primeval. How can I describe my home river in terms which plainly
show that all my close contact with the water has left me feeling, for
part of the time, that I am an outsider? I do not know, but I sometimes
feel it. The river can take on, especially in autumn and winter, an
identity hinted at by geologists – that it is a strand of a greater, long
lost, massive north sea river, and is a sister to the Rhine. Its other side
is so civilised, gentle, responsive to the arts of angling, sweet in water
and bank, that I can be persuaded that its darker side is an aberration
and think of Tweed as a reformed and civilised, even an enlightened
river. When it is being sweet, more than any other Scottish water it
deserves the abbeys on its banks. Indeed, it hints in those times of its
soft Saxon connections, when saintly men of Lindisfarne and York
chose it as a place to build monasteries, and villages with English greens
appeared in its valley. Then the river which I am beginning to feel
comfortable with changes again. Ettrick rises massively and carries a
bridge away. I find myself wading a well-known reach and feeling the
other wild river within plucking maliciously at my legs. I hook a
salmon which turns out to be unmanageable and after nearly all my
backing goes out it rolls, shows itself to be huge, red, large-kyped, then
breaks loose. This is no longer the river of gentle waving green weed
and of parr and trout popping up beside the buttercups. This is the
uncouth ogre of a river, which carries tree trunks and dead sheep down
on its brown floods.

I have not always lived on Tweedside, but I have accumulated thirty
years of experience of fishing the river, first from an Edinburgh base
and latterly from my home, close to the middle Tweed and the Teviot.
From there, over a short stretch of hill roads, I can reach my own beat
on the upper river at Scrogbank. Fishing the lower, middle or upper
section of the river is a question of calender and, on a day-to-day basis,
of water. Every spring for some years I have had early salmon fishing

either on a good beat of the middle river, where a friend has a let, or on the lower Tweed near Birgham. Opening the season on the middle river is always a lottery. If water levels will let you into the pools, there is every chance of a seven or eight pound springer. The problem, as I hint, is height of water. What the middle Tweed wants in early February is medium to lowish water after late winter floods. I have seen the river establish this pattern often. One February we were flooded off on the opening day, but a sudden hard frost dramatically reduced the level of the river from over six feet on the Floors gauge to four-feet-six. The colour on the first day was yellow and on the second a slightly clearer yellowish green – typical of winter floods with snow in them. I returned home after the first day of flood, hardly having wet a line and feeling despondent, to tie up for the next day three two-inch copper tubes, all mixed yellow, orange and black hair. The next day at four-and-a-half feet, I found all the pools still hopeless, but in behind the point where the boat was tied up, in a few square yards of sheltered water between the roaring main stream of the pool and the bank, I took two springers. Sometimes a heavy flood which seems to shut you out of the pool, actually brings the fish in to your feet.

In all but the heaviest water, I hate heavy two-inch tube flies. They are horrible to cast and, unless the stream is really powerful, they dredge and snag on the bottom. Brass or copper tubes of an inch-and-a-half or waddingtons of similar size are much more to my taste in spring and autumn. I also like, more and more, long unweighted poly-thene tubes like the remarkable Purple McBain or, indeed, any long, sinuous dark hair tube with a nice trailing profile and mobile tail. I do not like to fish fast sinking lines. I enjoy slow to middle-range sinking lines in size 10 or 11. I fish these slow-sinking lines in double taper form because I normally use the single spey cast and the bulk of the double taper body helps with the dynamics of this cast. Spey casting is very much concerned with drawing line off the water and forming a large loop which can be rolled out in the forward cast, plucking the fly off the water as it goes, making a hissing sound as it lifts line off the waters and shoots any slack you may have gathered in your hand. It is all one seamless action involving hand, body and rod – the wading, the lifting of the fly, the line caressing the water and the loop carrying a long line out to pop the fly into the stream at the fishiest of angles below you. I can feel the rhythm of spring fly fishing now as I write – the sunk line coming round slowly, hanging for a few seconds below me, then, gathering in some slack, I roll the line downstream and see the fly lifting out of the water. The rod comes up and across, moving with a shallow dip of the top like a crescent moon on its back. Then the thrust of the rod takes the line out in a large rolling arc with enough power to draw from my fingers the slack I have coiled there and plop the big fly into the stream to search out more lies. Part of our fly fishing is in the rhythms, the dynamics, the movements of arms and body. Were I not in waders thigh deep in the Tweed, I might even call this the dance of fly fishing!

It is my view that Tweed fishers in spring and autumn far too often believe that success lies with the heaviest flies and the fastest sinking lines. They are wrong. While there may be specific places where the fly must dive deep, the Tweed in spring and autumn will yield its fish well to flies sunk but swimming up. If I find that I am catching the bottom, unless I know that there is a special reason for it – a snagging rock or a ledge – I inevitably change to a lighter fly. In some autumn waters I have turned to unweighted tubes on Tweed, and I am not conscious that salmon prefer them less than bottom seeking weighted tubes, unless the water is very cold indeed.

Tweed normally produces small springers under nine pounds in weight. They are often like litter sisters. Occasionally one becomes conscious of another race of fish at the opening of the year, but it is the small springer which is typical. One February three of us had an interesting experience, almost like drawing a curtain of small fish away and revealing a different class and type of fish below. It was during a cold snowy opening week on a good middle Tweed beat above Kelso. We took six or seven small springers on our first few days. It was glorious. The sun shone and the river ran clean between glittering snowy banks which tinted orange as the sun went down in the late afternoon. There was a pause on the third day, as though there were no more small springers for us to take. That day, one rod brought in a spring fish of fifteen pounds. The following morning another mid-teens fish was taken, along with, I think, one small fresh fish. Then, fishing on our last day, well into a clear afternoon which promised hard frost and began to freeze the line in the rings of the rod, I was fishing from the boat, which allowed me to hang my inch-and-a-half wine and white tube over a deep lie, under a great tree. I had a long draw which felt like a good salmon and was into a solid fish which held deep. While it did not indulge in any acrobatics, it ran hard several times and, with the rod rings freezing up, giving line in the runs began to worry me and the boatman. At one point a little lollipop of ice from my top ring ran down the line towards the fish. Hasty clearing helped, but the fish had to be played out quite carefully because of its size. I was landed on the bank, where there was a certain amount of walking backwards and forwards with frozen rings and hasty and hazardous de-icing of the top ring during the end game. When the salmon eventually came ashore, it was seventeen-and-a-half pounds, twice as large as the average Tweed springer and with the two big fish taken earlier in the week, it showed us that a race of larger springers was in the water that February.

The smaller fish had come first to our flies, then the larger ones, lurking in the deep lies. They were darker fish than our small springers. The boatman thought they might have been what he called 'Christmas fish'. He was not so much referring to an actual date of running, as to a race of winter fish which sometimes show up in the first spring catches. They are becoming rarer. I have only had a scattering of such fish in the last ten years.

My best Tweed springer ever was a late one, taken on an early Easter week on Lower Birgham at the beginning of April on a small tube fly – twenty pounds, fresh and fat. The year was 1987. Whether in February or April, spring fish of this size are rare on Tweed. Lower Birgham has, as far the records show, never had another twenty pounder in spring. I hardly expect to better this as a Tweed springer, but I hope for the slightly more common springers in the teens among the smaller springers which are typical. These mid-teens springers are all the more marvellous because they are slightly rare.

Springers on Tweed run well into April, and in the past, in the 1960s, they used to bring good sport in April and May to the whole middle and part of the upper Tweed. Yair, above the Ettrick, has had its good May fishings in the past. So has Ashiestiel, but within the last decade anglers have, I think, accepted that the early and later spring runs are now largely composed of a race of Ettrick and Yarrow fish, and they do not run the Tweed above Boleside. Believing this can produce a kind of self-defeating philosophy. We do not fish for upper Tweed springers because we believe that they are absent. Thus none is ever taken and the downward spiral reinforces itself. When the spring runs come again to upper Tweed, who will discover them? Well, I hope I will, fishing Scrogbank, but I know I am lazy about covering the pools when for years nobody has taken a fish in the area before late summer.

On balance, I am basically apprehensive about Tweed springers. They seem to have left the 1980s on something of a downward cycle. That is the broad stock picture but in practice it may not be the angling one. We catch springers, or any other salmon, under conditions of having catchable stock in our pools, in fishable water. Even in years of low runs, many anglers can take a fish here or a couple there and, for them, this is success. Springers run in batches and a rod can have the day of his life on one bit of water while one pool downstream other rods are blank. I saw this in the late 1980s one February week when the rod on the pool above me took five one morning while I touched nothing. We changed places at lunch and he again took two and I found the top pool to be empty. Batches or pockets of fish typify a poorly stocked river, yet they can bring memorable sport to a given beat or a given pool. Looking at the situation on the whole river, however, I find myself very uneasy when its spring pools are empty save for the passing trade of runners.

I am also apprehensive about summer runs into Tweed in recent
years. The late spring and early summer can sometimes bring good
sport to the middle river and the Ettrick. But Tweed summer salmon
used to be an important feature on the upper river also. In the early
1960s, when I was new to the Tweed, a Somerset friend of mine took
fishings in August on Ashiestiel, several miles above the junction with
the Ettrick. He had lowish water, but, finding salmon in some of the
pools he decided to fish a tiny devon upstream, bringing the bait down
at high speed over the salmon. He took, I think, five for his week and
all were good, fresh or fairly fresh summer salmon. I joined him and
lost a salmon on the fly there too. There is no doubt that a run of good
summer salmon in the 1960s and 1970s came into Tweed beats, but there
is also little doubt that it has declined and in the upper Tweed has all
but disappeared. I am also apprehensive that the grilse runs we used to
fish for in July and August and into September, have declined, one
hopes only temporarily. The end of the 1980s was a particularly worrying time for its loss of grilse. One argument is the estuary nets and the
former river netting stations virtually netted out the runs of summer
salmon and grilse, except in times of flood. There is some substance in
this complaint, and when the Atlantic Salmon Conservation Trust
acted, with great foresight, to buy out almost all of the river nets in the
late 1980s, we hoped for an improvement in summer catches. The taking
off of the nets, however, coincided with two of the worst drought years
we have had in recent times and the pattern of the summer has remained
dismal. One of the hopes we all cherish, is that, through excellent
management policies like taking off river nets and the proposed taking
off of estuary nets at Tweedmouth, the summer Tweed will again yield
good salmon and grilse. On a broader front, the loss of grilse has been
reported quite widely throughout Scotland, on the North and South
Esk in Angus, on the Dee and on other northern east-flowing rivers. It
is disturbing. To lose grilse suggests that we might be losing a whole
generation of salmon in a given year. It is not just that some grilse may
be expected to survive spawning and return to the river as heavier
summer salmon in future years. It is the thought that the grilse may
have been lost either by almost total predation or interceptory netting at
sea or in the estuary. Worse, they might have succumbed to an environmental disaster, say to do with changes in sea feeding. We have seen
what may be environmental changes badly affecting stocks of west
coast Irish and Scottish sea trout. We are faced with global climatic
changes, actual and threatened, and it is extremely worrying that
comparatively small changes in sea temperature may have radical
consequences for salmon, and sea trout, sea feeding. One or two years
of low catches do not make a disaster, of course, especially when water
levels were poor on many east coast Scottish rivers in the summers

of the late 1980s. But I feel worried, and will be looking carefully at the Tweed's performance in the 1990s. I hope I see a revival of both summer salmon and grilse. The river needs them badly.

It is, of course, the autumn which gives the Tweed its celebrated name. The Tweed can be a prodigious salmon river from September onwards. A whole new race of larger salmon, sometimes in great numbers, runs the river and, according to water, produces sport in any or all of the three sections of the Tweed and in its tributaries. In most years, how the autumn runs are shared out over the whole river is a question of water. Low water in September and early October usually means that the river below Kelso, including the killing grounds of the Junction Pool, do well. Fish can pack the lower river in tens of thousands. There is, of course, a huge annual lottery for Tweed fishers on how the autumn floods are distributed. If there is high water in late September and early October, the lower river can be washed out and the middle and the upper Tweed can have magnificent sport. Normally, the first autumn fish stock the lower and middle river to Boleside and, if water is right, they run the Ettrick and Yarrow. This can result in Boleside having some concentrated, not to say hectic sport. Fresh run fish, some with sea lice on them, might well be taken in the Tweed above Ettrick from late August onwards, and in wet summers grilse and small summer fish do give good sport there, but it is the beginning of October really, before the upper Tweed gets its stock. Waves of fish arrive. You can easily identify the fresh, fast running summer grilse and small salmon, silvery, sprightly, fast. Usually, they are followed by coloured fish from the lower and middle river, salmon which have been residents there for weeks and have run on with the coming of the water. Then come the true autumn fish, the larger, greyer salmon, cocks of eighteen to thirty pounds, hens in the upper teens, coarser in scale than springers or summer fish, larger in mouth and head, great, heaving strong-tailed fish which pull like horses.

October and early November days on middle and upper Tweed can be wild, with high water, wind, even snow. But the sport in the autumn water can be marvellous, with fish pulling hard at the fly and giving a tremendous account of themselves in the heavy streams. Tweed can exceed all your superlatives in autumn, and can bring clean fish to the fly until the last day of November, and no doubt on every day of the close season during the winter, if it were legal to fish.

There can be some prodigious catches on the right water and the right day. Most of the larger fisheries can produce lists of anglers who have had ten salmon to their own rod in a day. Twice in the 1980s I had the good luck to join the double figure club, once on Boleside and once on Lower Floors, but for me as for many other Tweed anglers there have been lucky days over the years with multiple fish, days when the

sport seemed continuous, days when it was almost impossible to put
the fly into the river without something pulling it. On the biggest
autumn days you might find yourself hooking, playing, selecting and
returning fish constantly. These days are times we all dream about
and long for, but it is interesting that, when they actually happen, they
are strange events. Moreover, after they have happened, for me at least,
they are difficult days to live with. After two really big days at the end
of one Tweed season, I felt a distinct inhibition in my fishing for the
first half of the next year. I felt that, like a starving man, I had been
invited to a banquet, had gorged myself, and as a result had ruined my
stomach. I have often written about the exhilaration of salmon fishing
and I have reported success as part of that. But there are many dimensions in success. Catching salmon is a special kind of quest. It is an
operation, like all hunting, in which the difficulty of locating the game
and outwitting it is the essence of the sport. Success is only valued
because it is achieved against difficulty or adversity. Catching five fish
every day, without difficulty, would turn me into a golfer. It is the
struggle which avails. Perhaps I should say that, just to keep things in a
decent perspective, I am no stranger to the blank week, and, indeed, in
one recent autumn, despite good water and a resonable number of days
out on the upper river, I was blank throughout October and November
on Tweed.

The autumn harvest on Tweed is very varied. One day you have
a brace of silvery seven-pounders and another, you catch and return a
sixteen-pound hen, well coloured and full of roe, or take a twenty-
pound cock after a long struggle. Along with the fresh and not so fresh
salmon, small and large, autumn on Tweed can produce some most
interesting sea trout. These fish are special to the Tweed and the type is
shared by a few neighbouring rivers in Scotland and in Northumbria.
They are often large fish, ten pounds or over, darkish in colour, even
when completely fresh. I have had one of nine-and-a-half pounds and
several not much smaller. Colleagues have, over the years, had sea trout
from six to thirteen-and-a-half pounds. Fish in double figures are
reported every autumn. The record British sea trout was, I believe, one
of twenty pounds taken in autumn in the 1980s from Tweed at Peebles,
fifty miles from the sea. We see numbers of sea trout showing in
autumn in Tweed and certain beats have streams and pools well known
for holding them, usually associated with spawning burns. Yet, despite
their numbers, only a small proportion of these sea trout are taken.
These special North Sea fish remind us that rivers not only have species
of fish in them but also races of these fish with genetic characteristics.
They are races with typical growth rates, dates of migration, destina-
tions and spawning behaviour. Tweed sea trout do not contribute much
to the fishing fame of the main river, although they are highly valued

on the Till, a Northumbrian tributary of the lower Tweed. Tweed sea trout are often spoken about as curiosities. On some beats, they are regarded as inferior to salmon. Some ghillies call them 'Sea dogs'. I certainly do not like hooking small black Tweed sea trout on the salmon rod in autumn when I have my eye on a fresh salmon showing in a lie, but I am, nevertheless, full of awe for the larger sea trout, and am often stunned by their power. I do not rate these late sea trout as good table fish, but I have several friends who say the larger fish smoke splendidly and have a finer texture of flesh than salmon.

I hope these special Tweed sea trout are not on the danger list, but I have noticed with concern catches of large Tweed sea trout, six to twelve pounds in weight, which have recently appeared on Edinburgh fishmongers' slabs. These come from the Farne Islands and are part of the Northumbrian fishery, which includes drift nets. This drift net fishery is a gross anomaly, taking large numbers of salmon and sea trout returning to the Tweed (and other eastern Scottish waters), operating, at the time of writing, under an unreformed English law which allows drift net fishing off the English coast. In Scotland, drift nets were banished in the early 1960s and, internationally, are now denounced and are banned in more and more coastal and open waters worldwide. It is ridiculous that this English fishery should reap its harvest from fish bred in and returning to a Scottish river. Vigorous efforts are being made to deal with this problem and a phasing out is proposed. I profoundly hope that the solution does not come too late for the Tweed, where, despite radical improvements in the river netting scene, and proposed for the estuary netting operation, and an excellent organisation for protecting the spawning and nursery aspects of the salmon in freshwater, up to 70,000 salmon can be taken annually at sea by the adjacent North-East drift netting operation in Northumberland seriously threatening the river.

The Tweed has undoubtedly played an important part in shaping me as a salmon and trout fisher. I see the river almost daily. Like Eliot's archetypal river, the rhythms of the Tweed are present in my life. I walk to the bottom of the field in front of my house and see a spring which swells the local burn, whose waters run into Ale, then Teviot, then Tweed. On Tweed itself, I know at a glance, pausing to look over this bridge or that, exactly how high or low it is running. Even as I drive, catching glimpses of the river, it gives me glints of colour and patterns of wind which are meaningful signs to me as a fisher. As if it had special magnetism, the Tweed draws me to its banks and involves me in its flow, its fish, its trees, its bankside life. It always seems to me to be a knowing river, conscious of its own long and rich human history as well as its gripping presence in the natural landscape. I love Tweed lore – ballads, histories and above all, accounts of the river as a fishing water of distinction. I relish the delightful Scrope, the gripping Stoddart and the lyrical and rambling Lang brothers. Scott's presence is stamped everywhere, of course, and it has given me much satisfaction to take salmon from the pools on the doorstep of both Ashiestiel and Abbotsford where he fished. Yet despite all this excellent documentation, despite all its luring and embracing, the Tweed is, for me, still something of an unknown river. At times I would almost say it was arcane. It has secrets which no amount of my walking its banks, or fishing its pools has allowed me to penetrate. Perhaps the Tweed is reminding me that the essence of any river is contained not so much in what you can document about it, but in how well you are in tune with it. Tweed brings together hills and high moors which I love, timbered banks which I delight in, great sweeps of pastures filled with sheep and the inscrutable North Sea with which its waters merge. I suspect that the unknown Tweed, with its special races of fish, is kin to that sea and it is this which makes me aware of its hidden character. In this light, the Tweed is not restricted to three great parts; it has four, and the fourth is the North Sea itself.

CHAPTER
10

A special kind of greatness

I FISHED THE TAY REGULARLY for something like twenty-five years, fishing mainly the middle reaches near Caputh but often getting the chance to fish the fat lower river from Stanley to Almondmouth. I loved the range of the fishings – from chilling January openings through the spring weeks, into the Tay's undervalued summer with chance good days with salmon, grilse – and sometimes sea trout – and fat days in autumn. Then, for no very good reason, for several years I was virtually separated from the river. Quite unexpectedly I was recently invited by a friend to fish Taymount in January and I returned, conscious of two strong feelings. Firstly, that I somehow owed the river an apology for being away. Secondly, I realised on my first day back that I had almost forgotten something I learned early in my Tay years – that this memorable river is not one water; it is a complex experience, a kind of Chinese box with a river within a river within a river.

That early season visit to Taymount illustrated this well. Taymount was new to me. I had in fact never fished this splendid beat before, although I had many times fished below and above it. I therefore thought I knew more or less what to expect. I turned down the wood-land track which led to the river and looked through the trees at the water on my right and suffered something like culture shock. The Tay bowled me over. It was absolutely magnificent. The January river was running high, eight feet on the gauge, but it was running clear as the Tay often does, reminding us of the Grampian hinterland of the river with its hard bedrock, its scoured valleys and that vast clear reservoir, Loch Tay, filling a great glen above. Taymount looked like a Wagnerian stage set. Geologically the beat is spectacular. At the lower end of Tay-mount a ridge of the Highland Line crosses the river – that great geological fault which runs from the North Sea at Stonehaven diagonally south west over the country to meet the sea again in Argyll. The Highland line is more than a signficant feature of landscape, however. It runs like an endless wall to the north-west of the Lowlands separating with its scarp the lands of raspberries and wheat from the Highlands beyond, announcing the end of one world and the beginning of another – mountainous, often harsh, enigmatic, serene. No traveller, whether he is a fisher or not, can fail to sense the changes which that line announces. The river, over aeons of time, has breached the fault, pouring through it in a series of fine rapids and pools. It has cut its spectacular way through the ridge at Taymount and has gouged out below it a pool which the boatmen say categorically is 120 feet deep.

Below the Taymount ridge, the river opens out into a broad valley, rich with oak and beech. It weaves broad streams beside wide shingles, forms famous pools above and below Stanley then eases its pace as it approaches Scone, Perth and the long estuary below. The Taymount ridge hems the beat in between steep banks, mounds of enormous glaciated boulders, old pine trees, ash, rowan and larch. There, the river is shaped into a series of wide streams and long gliding pools with rugged banks where pines stand columnar on the tops of shattered grey rocks. At the top end of Taymount home beat, the river broadens out to form comparatively shallow streams which run in complex patterns over rocks and shingle to produce a river a hundred yards wide. On my January visit, much of this wide streamy water broke white over rocks, but dark runs with glassy patches swept under the high banks, looking excellent for the big spring fly.

I wanted to fly fish, eight feet of January water or not, and I was fully expecting the boatmen to say I was mad. Tay boatmen have often been rather direct about this in the past, when I said I would rather not spin and did not really want to harl from the boats. 'Daft! Naebody fishes the flee here till June', they would say, tapping their foreheads with their fingers knowingly, when they thought I was out of sight.

That day the diagnosis was different, since the head ghillie turned out to be an old friend from years before on the Tweed, John Lindsay, an excellent fly fisher. He stooped down and drew a little map for me on the sand: 'Go up to the top of the lower beat, down the steps at the third path, walk or wade up past the rocks to the landslip and try to go upstream of that. Fish past the old ash trees back to the steps down to the Stobhall boat and let your fly come well into your own side.'

I managed to get past the landslip, looked down at the water I was to cover and saw a series of streams with long scalloped edges and a cliffy bank rising through trees immediately behind. I love these banks with little bays and points. They always indicate lies just off them where the bed of the river takes up the story of the bank. At that height of water, of course, I was fishing my fly where, in later spring and summer, fishers would sit and picnic. I was, as a boatman once said on Redgorton', 'looking for salmon on the footpath'. I selected a big two-and-a-half-inch Brora waddington Willie Gunn, set up my heaviest rod and began rolling out the fly into the turbulence of the stream, trying to let the big fly hover and dangle in the sheltered water inside the main rush. It felt all wrong. The heavy rod would not work well. The fly kept finding the river bed and it refused to hang nicely in the gentler water. I reeled in, set up my sweet fifteen-foot Mackenzie Philps rod, chose an inch-and-a-half Orange and Black waddington, far lighter than the big Brora I had been wrestling with, waded in, got my single spey cast working well and felt better about everything. I saw two fish splashing at the steps, probably big kelts, but I moved down to them and, standing under a crooked ash tree above them, I had a splendid take – a strong, determined pull which made the reel go, then a heavy pulsing run out into the stream and up through it into the fast water above. Could it be a springer? I couldn't see the fish. Was it possible? Why wouldn't it come nearer into the gentler water? If it wasn't a springer, it was a very powerful fish, definitely not kelt-like. This anxious and exciting debate went on for more than ten minutes, during which I began to sense that I was in fact into a very large, strong kelt, not a fresh fish, but a goer of the first order, taking line and running well. I have had kelts like this before – real stormers. When the fish came in, I tailed it and had difficulty getting my hand round the 'wrist' above the tail because of its size. It was a solid, good-looking fish which in my hand as I released it, felt nearer twenty pounds than fifteen. In length and bone it must have been in the mid-twenties when it was fresh. It may seem strange to many of my colleagues that I welcomed that first kelt, and, in a way, I felt welcomed by it. It was so typically a Tay fish. I felt I was back in Tay business, back to the twenty-five years of excellent fishing I had had on the river before I began neglecting it.

The scalloped bank near the path with the steps went on making me feel as if I was back home. I had three more kelts in quick succession, then a lost fish which was probably another. Finally, I had a pull from a fish which felt different. A small fish, a strong salmon, not knocking like a kelt, but pulling out into the stream in a more determined way. I glimpsed a high back, and a good tail and a couple of circles later I drew the fish to the bank. It was not a kelt. It was a seven-pound, well-shaped, little salmon, bluish-silver, clean in the gills, most certainly not a spawned fish, but in my hand it felt full, not the tight bar of muscle a fresh January springer would have been. It was probably a baggot, a fish which has for some reason retained its eggs, perhaps to reabsorb them. I have only ever caught fish of this type and colour on the Tay. Or, possibly, this little salmon might have been a winter fish which would still spawn. The Tay has races of fish which appear only in the winter and spawn in the winter–spring. My little fish was perhaps not a residue from the autumn. I was sorry it was not a springer, as I returned it and saw it speed away. Going back to the hut with a fly-caught springer in January would have been wonderful. As it was, I had had an hour and a half of excitement, pulls, runs, large kelts and small ones, a lost fish and a baggot.

I sometimes think about the issue that all the pleasures of fishing seem to culminate in knocking a fish on the head. Isn't the killing of the fish the evidence that your fishing has been successful and satisfying? The longer I fish, the less this is true for me. Of course, there is a great feeling of success in taking a well-coloured, well-shaped salmon, showing it to your friends, entering it in the book in the hut, photographing it, admiring it, remembering it. But, is this a necessary end to the chain of pleasure – reading the water, selecting the tackle, casting well, getting pulls and plucks, hooking the fish and bending the rod in the fight? I believe the skills and satisfactions of fishing are separate from the killing of the fish, although, on many occasions bringing the fish home adds pleasure to pleasure. I felt, on that January Tay day, that I had had all the pleasure of fishing, yet every fish had had to be returned. I do not deny that, had the little baggot been a springer, I would have taken it home. That Tay day was great fishing, even if the book says we were blank. For me it was the Tay revisited, majestic, exciting, impressive. After my separation from it, I experienced again the ineffable contact with the river itself in its daunting high water spring persona.

My earlier years on the Tay were fervent ones. I chose Perth as the first city I taught in, partly because of the Tay and the Earn, its tributary, which flowed near my home in Auchterarder. When I moved to Edinburgh, I found a group of friends who fished a beat of the middle Tay, Burnbane, on Saturdays, and this became my home water. The fat beats of lower Tay identifed three parts of the fishing year, spring which ended in early May when the boats were taken off the river, autumn which brought very productive fishing especially on the lower river from the end of August onwards to mid-October, and the so-called unproductive summer in between. From our less auspicious banks at Burnbane, we saw the year differently. We fished hard in the spring and caught what we could by spinning and fly fishing from the bank, including a thirty-eight-and-a-half-pounder taken by a friend early one March. But we had lovely warm weather fishing there in May, June and July, much of it fly fishing, and in quality every bit as good as the sport of the spring. The autumn for us in the Caputh area was productive, but it did not yield the mass of fish which lower beats like Benchil and Islamouth showed in September and October. Many of our September fish at Burnbane were coloured, but a good proportion were strong, silver fish straight from the sea. One or two of our October salmon were winter-springers, fish which would possibly run up to Loch Tay and provide the earliest spring catch there. The river seemed to me to have an almost endless series of races of salmon, including winter fish which anglers hardly see, except perhaps as chance fish in the closing days of the season in mid-October, or as bluish springers in the earliest days of the next.

We comforted ourselves at Burnbane, by looking upstream from Caputh bridge to the small cottage where Miss Ballantyne lived, the lady who, fishing the pool immediately in front of her small house in the autumn of 1922, hooked and landed the British record salmon of sixty four pounds. She was still alive when I first fished at Burnbane. I saw her once in her garden, but I never called on her. I regret this very much. She was not only the record holder, with a fish which has not been surpassed for size in Britain since its capture in 1922, she was also a link with a past Tay world, with large estates intact, boats held against the river by double boatmen, flies dressed on large single irons, spinning done precariously with fresh and preserved sprats, loaches, or what seem now seem weird artificials like phantom devons and wagtails.

On Burnbane, the river within the river was very apparent. As the water fell, the first sign was that the main pool shrank and its glides became sluggish. The best lies in the stream were found further and further up under what would have been unfishable runs in spring. Further drought let us wade out to reach lies normally protected by powerful unwadeable glides. I remember a July day of this, wading where no boot had waded before that year, leaning precariously, despite the low river, on tons of pushing water as I edged out. Then, casting my longest line with a size six shrimp, taking two splendid salmon from behind a sunk boulder at the tail of Sparrowmuir. Even when its bones were showing, the Tay was a mighty river within a river. At the other end, when it flooded spectacularly with ten or twelve feet of clear water, and forced us to cling to the high banks and fish, as it were, a new river, we could take salmon from flooded back-waters and eddies while the river roared past unfishable. The Tay is a complex of rivers on any beat, as I was reminded on my January day at Taymount. At each height, you put a new template over its flow and find new streams and new lies. I love looking for salmon 'on the path', but I love even more the new streams and runs and lies which low water creates. I like the feeling that drought lets us go inside the Tay to the river within. I love the long wading over the shingles, discovering as I go the shape and nature of the bed normally concealed from us by high water, discovering runnels, streams and potholes in the new, low river and taking salmon from them on small flies and a floating line.

My separation from the Tay was partly geographical, since I moved to the Borders, but partly because I had a growing dislike for the Tay style of boat fishing. Tay boats harl the pools. That is, they weave back and forth and trail behind them two or even three baits, like Tay lures or Kynoch Killers (large plastic wobbling plugs), tobies, and sometimes flies. It is, of course exciting to see your rod, or at any rate one of the three propped over the stern, twitching, pulling or jigging as a fish takes. There is an urgency then to grab it, bend into the fish, come to terms with it and be taken ashore to play and land it. But where is the casting, the reading of the water, the contact with the taking fish? Why did the fish select that particular lure? How can fishers settle for a mode of fishing in which they give up the feeling of the rod in the hand, the rhythm of presenting fly or bait, the judgement of where and how to cover the water and above all, give up the first fine rapture of contact, the first thrilling moment of the take? I fish from boats on all sorts of rivers, but I cast from them. On Tay, it is the boatman and his motor which harls the bait and, immobile and often cold in the boat, two anglers sit, talking, having a glass of whisky, looking at the river, the trees, the rocks, perhaps even thinking about their bank balances, while the boat crosses and re-crosses the holding water and fishes the Tay on their behalf. No! I will not allow a Tay boat to become my fishing proxy.

Tay, like Tweed, is also a system of tributaries and several of them are very unlike the main river. The Earn and Isla, for example, are slow streams; the Tummel is open and streamy over its lower few miles but it is truncated by the Faskally hydro–dam, and above that it is a decapitated river, with its tributary the Garry just a desert, starved of water. I never fished the Tummel or Garry before the dam came. I have talked to one of the former owners, however, now a Dee proprietor, and he has spoken of the marvellous Highland pools of the old Faskally. He commissioned a series of watercolours of the old pools before the dam blotted them out. There they are, gorges, deep runs, glides and pot-holes under craggy rocks and pine-clad banks. The Tummel, of course, still fishes, and can be rewarding water. Salmon do ascend the fish ladder at the dam, although the count seems to be endlessly down on previous years. Immediately below the dam the Tummel can sometimes be spectacular, but the whole Tummel–Garry system is a testimony to the false proposition that we had to sacrifice our priceless natural environment to produce power. The proposition was false, mainly because it assumed that we had the right to make irreversible changes to the Highlands in the name of cheap power. It was also false in its economics; hydro power is not cheap, and in terms of national grid demands is trivial. The hydro-electric movement was also a primitive one which did not have any formula for calculating the value, in environmental terms, of the landscape and resources it was blotting out. What a loss was there, my countrymen!

The Garry above, while it still runs late salmon, ironically came into my ken first when, as a university geography student, I was introduced to its extraordinary potholed bed, now exposed and dry. What a place for salmon it must have been! It must also have been the most difficult and subtle water on which to fish a fly. The rock formations of the bed were dramatic enough before the water sculpted them to produce gullies and sudden hollows up to eight feet deep, and quite extra-ordinary, almost perpendicular cylindrical holes scoured out by the endless action of boulders turned within them by the stream. Seeing the bed of the dried-out Garry is not how I want to discover the river within a river, but it reveals dramatically some of the hidden features which contribute to the character of any water. What it does not show, however, is how the water and the rock marry. Only the salmon know that.

I got to know parts of the Earn well when I lived in that part of Perthshire. This Lowland river, slow in its lower reaches, deep and strange in places, is an excellent trout stream, has or had good sea trout and shared the spring and autumn runs of the Tay. I never got to know the Isla, that other gentle, very un-Highland looking tributary which comes in from the north east and is joined by the more Highland Ericht and Ardle near Coupar Angus. Again it is a good trout and grayling stream. It is not regarded highly as a salmon river, but it has given its name to a famous salmon beat, Islamouth, where you can find some of the best autumn fly fishing glides on the whole Tay system.

As a trout fisher, especially in the days before I could afford salmon fishing on the better waters, I used to envy salmon fishers their sport. On several occasions on Tay, however, this envy has been reversed. I remember one May day at Stenton when the salmon rods were all blank. I met on the banks of Willie's Hole a Murthly trout fisher, working his way up the glides with a dry fly. We talked. He opened his bag and inside he had at least a dozen trout and four of them were over two pounds. It was the finest bag of wild trout I think I have ever seen from a Scottish river. He was a superb fly fisher and a fine sportsman. In comparison to his dry fly trout rod, my fifteen-foot fly rod seemed like a tree, and my flies and casts appeared coarse. Meeting that fisher reminded me that the Tay was, and still is, an excellent trout water and is capable of producing sport to the dry fly and nymph which few rivers in Scotland can match. The trout river within the salmon river is another aspect of the Tay being a complex of waters.

If I were asked to choose one of these rivers within the Tay, which would it be? Heaven forfend! I hope I never have to make the choice. Would it be the dark, full river of spring, with all the difficulties of covering the lies, but all the force of the water adding to the fight with hooked fish? The scenario for the spring river is fishing the scalloped bank of Burnbane stream with a fly in early February and taking a fifteen-pounder. Would my choice be the sweeter May river, popping with trout as well as salmon? May can produce days like one on Stenton when I had been delayed and arrived to find the boat ashore and the boat and bank rods having what they called a late breakfast. Everybody looked disappointed, for they had toiled from early morning and taken nothing. I put up my fly rod, waded to the island and crossed it to the Island Pool beyond. Under the boughs of an oak tree at the tail I saw a small splash, fished down to it and had a twelve-pounder, absolutely shining fresh, and so covered in sea lice, long and short tailed, that my friend Ian Calcott counted them – twenty eight. Or would my day be in June or July when the river drops away and the summer Tay within the spring Tay can be discovered? Perhaps they would be like the summer days on Sparrowmuir pool at Burnbane when we waded to hitherto unreachable lies and found them full of fish which swept and bulged at the fly and pulled hard. Or would it be a late summer evening described by Jim Fisher on the thin chuckling streams of Taymount, when he took three from one small streamy lie and went on to make the bag five before dusk, all on small flies, from lies in the fine streamy water which in a higher river lie masked. Perhaps it would be to enjoy still later riches – the Tay in late summer and early autumn at Almondmouth or Benchil when the small fly and the floating line is in business all day with masses of fish which have run up after the estuary nets are taken off for the season. No, I cannot decide. The Tay has all the elements of being an embarrassment of riches. It would be better, if I absolutely had to choose one day and walk the plank afterwards, to settle for the Tay tomorrow, taking it just as it comes. You would never know which of the rivers within the Tay you would find, but each would be rich with its own possibilities. No matter the height, the Tay, to the right eye is always that special kind of paradox, which Homer identifies in the Grecian sea – always different, always the same, *einfach*, with a special kind of greatness.

CHAPTER

11

The trout of the Pindus

I HAD THE GREAT FORTUNE in the early 1970s to work for two years in Greece and to travel widely through the country while I was there. Indeed, by a stroke of irony, although it was a time of great restriction under the military regime of the Colonels, I was able to travel freely in areas which were normally closed. My post in the British Council was technically on the staff of the Cultural Attaché of the British Embassy and in this role I had a white diplomatic identity card which gave me wide freedom to travel in the course of my work in Greece. You might wonder what this had to do with trout fishing. In the end, it was vital to it, because my search for Greek trout kept pointing to the rivers of the Pindus mountains as the most likely home of catchable trout and they form part of the north-west frontier of Greece.

The area I particularly wanted to visit was the Epirus, the north-western corner of Greece, and the rivers which I heard about and read about seemed all to be the headwaters in Greece of rivers which flowed on through Albania. Along the frontier with Albania there was a controlled military zone and only those with special passes were allowed into it. That was where the white card scored. The military commander of the area allowed me to move about freely in the area and the local police checkpoints not only regarded me as *persona grata* but also enthusiastically helped me to find my way around, and told me stories of great trout lying in green pools in the waters I was to fish. Not all of these stories were apocryphal. Some of the rivers of the Epirus were, for all practical purposes, closed waters. A kind of artificial trout sanctuary had been formed by the military zone, protecting the trout, among other things, from the Albanians, but no less from certain Greek fishers, whose

main technique seemed to be using gelignite. I was, therefore, able to
fish some of the rivers of this wonderful region in what angling history
might record as the post-gelignite era, and in a memorable way it gave
me an insight into what the fishings in the Pindus rivers must have been
in the pre-gelignite age.

Every fishing expedition begins with talk. The cynical might say that
fishing ends with talk too – that, indeed, fishing is a kind of sandwich
of stories, before and after, with a thin filling of activity in the middle.
I certainly asked a lot of questions in Athens before my first trip to the
Pindus. Perhaps I sometimes asked the wrong people, because my
questions got some curious answers. I came across numbers of people
who hardly knew the word *pestrophes* (trout). Indeed, I began at times
to wonder whether Greeks knew anything about their own natural
environment. Perhaps I was unlucky, or naive to expect the people
I met in salons in Athens to know what a tree was, or a fish or a bird.
Conversations of the most zany kind stick in my memory.

'Can you tell me what that is?' I said indicating a tree we could see.

'It's a tree.'

'Yes, sure. But what kind of tree?'

'Oh, it's just a tree.'

'No, no. I mean what *type* of tree?' I said, pressing my Greek into
forming a more specific question.

There was some blankness, then some gestures.

'Ah, I know what you mean', said one. 'There are olive trees and
others, and that's an other!'

Laughter. But it was laughter which in this and other conversations
made me wonder if anybody really knew about animals and trees and
fish. Indeed, I wondered whether this ignorance of the environment
came from the top, because, while I was in Greece, one of the Colonels,
Patakos, made a speech about the beauty of Greece in which he claimed
that there was no pollution in the Greek air and that the Greek seas
were pure. There is wonderful unpolluted air in much of Greece, but
you have only to sail in to Piraeus to see Athens lying as if in a divine
dish lipped by its mountains, and to notice that the dish is overflowing
with a yellow fog. You have only to sit on an Aegean beach, looking at
perfect islands with pines down to the shore, and to discover that you
have sat in a patch of oil, to lose something of the romance of the day.

Sometimes my questions about trout produced what amounted to
proverbs in reply. One of these, which I heard several times, was:
'There are no trout in the rivers which flow east'. That's a lot of water!
If you think of Greece (excluding the Peloponnese) the Pindus mountain range, which forms the spine of the country, lies over to the west
coast. There are rivers from the Pindus flowing east over the plain of
Thessalay, for example, and there are rivers of the north flowing into the

Aegean, which I find it hard to believe have no trout in them, even in their mountain headwaters. For example, the older guide books and some travel accounts which I had read mentioned trout in the rivers of the meteora country – the spectacular region of abrupt, cliffy hills, like volcanic stubs, some with monasteries perched on top, in the area of Thessalay between Trikkala and Kalambaka. This lay on my route to the north west and I decided to ask locally on my way whether there were trout in the area. At Kalambaka, for example, the Pinios looked as though it should hold trout, but locally they said there were none. They spoke of there being good trout in the Aspro Potami to the west of Kalambaka, but I did not manage to get over to this valley, which, in any case, turned out to be the the headwaters of one of the largest of the Pindus rivers, the Acheloos, which flows south and west to join the Ionian sea 200 miles to the south. The proverb was proving to be true. I suspect that the absence of trout from the rivers flowing east from the Pindus is simply a matter of access. These rivers flow through more gentle and more populated country than the western rivers and it would not surprise me to find that they have merely been fished out. Even the western waters of the Pindus, where there is easy access, are either fished out or were in the course of being so when I was there.

This was well illustrated when I was crossing the Pindus on the magnificent mountain road from Kalambaka up to the east–west watershed at the Pass of Katra then down the cliffy valley with a western-flowing torrent beside the road to Metsovon and on towards Joannina. The road crossed a lovely looking mountain stream, the Zagoritikos. I stopped and walked down by its streams, then set up my trout rod and fished a run here and pool there. I had a rise, then another and this time hooked a small whitefish, then another. None of the rises produced trout. I walked on, casting here and there and came upon a Greek man fishing a handnet. His technique was fascinating. He was wading upstream and he would position his handnet below a boulder, push the boulder over with his foot and after a short pause, lift out his net. I don't know whether he felt the fish go into the net, as the Solway haaf netters do with salmon in the flowing tide, but he caught several fish while I was watching, all whitefish.

'Are there other fish here too?' I asked.

'Sure! There are chub and catfish.'

'And trout?' I asked. 'Oh yes, there are some trout. There are traps for trout and whitefish downstream of here. I don't catch many here, though. There aren't as many as there used to be.'

At this point he caught a couple of tiny whitefish and popped them into his basket.

'Why do you kill such little fish?' I asked.

'Oh they're the sweetest', he replied disarmingly. I thought of a line in one of Lawrence's essays on the shooting of song birds in Italy: 'But imagine the small mouthful of little bones each of these tiny carcasses must make!'. Had the trout all been netted out as fingerlings and mixed with tiddler whitefish, chub and catfish, been scrunched as succulent *marithes* (minnows)? I asked him about returning small fish and conserving the stock, if only to get more sizeable fish in the crop. But the idea found no favour. He thought others would just take advantage. I didn't go on to suggest that the most valuable crop of all might be to catch trout on fly in a lovely river like this. I didn't argue that people would pay to do this, would rent rooms, would buy petrol and food and welly boots and that a pound of trout caught on the fly would be worth perhaps a hundred times the value of a pound of trout trapped in the wild. Maybe my arguments would be wrong. Perhaps a netted-out river with its miserable crop of minnows is in a kind of natural balance, while my sporting stream would be an artificial interference. He believed strongly that rivers were for food, natural bounty, where you could use your net, or a trap, or for that matter your hand grenade, and, as long as the natural stock lasted, you could win a free meal or two or make a few drachmas. I watched him for some time. He was extremely skilled. He could handle his net deftly and delicately and, more important, he could read every stream perfectly, like the very best fly fisher. He obviously loved the water, the fish, the catches. Switch him to a slightly different wavelength, I thought, and he would make a brilliant trout fisher.

I made Joannina my base and there negotiated a pass to allow me to drive up the road which runs north from the town parallel with the mountains which lie to the east. At the check point at Kalpakion, where the road to Albania forks left to the frontier about twelve miles distant, I took the road to Konitsa and began to travel through some remarkable country. This is the area which carries the headstreams of rivers which cross the Albanian border and reach the sea eventually north-east of Corfu. These rivers of the northern Pindus are incredibly beautiful. They carve their way through some of the loveliest scenery in Europe. The road from Kalpakion climbs to a mountain pass and from the top an absolutely breathtaking view unrolls. To the right are the tremendous cliffs of the Pindus, with the high tops behind, reaching 8,000 feet. Below the tops, on the high plateaux, rivers cut spectacular gorges. This is soluble limestone country, like the Cévennes of southern France or the *karst* country of the Dalmatian coast of Jugoslavia, but more spectacular. Through this fantastic area, water and weather cut gorges, carve pillars, and etch ledges in a fantastic display of what seems more like architecture than natural scenery. The rivers overwhelm you with their sculpted courses. They surge into caves and pour down potholes;

they eddy into peach and white basins and they run clear over shallows and green over depths in streams, pools and cascades. It is natural that your eye would be arrested by the brilliance of the surface of the land-scape which lies before you, but in this region there is that most gripping of all phenomena, rivers underground, rivers lurking in caverns, carving dark caves just as elaborate as the surface ones, gliding past pillars and dripping stalactites, forming who knows what pools and lakes and streams in that subterranean place and emerging, still with a whiff of the underworld, to scour deep pools and flow green and deep and divine, barely concealing the shapes of the trout lurking in their waters.

The Voithamatis, the principal trout river of this region, was one of these limestone waters. From a distance, you can see the river emerging from its gorge in the mountains and below the high gorge, with its limestone pools and streams and cliffy banks with their church-like columns and grottos, it emerges from the highlands to wind over a stony plain and join the distant Aoos. Beyond this, a dozen miles away to the north west, are the mountains of Albania, a gripping, mysterious looking place. What streams lie there? What uncharted waters? What trout lurk in these pools? The whole setting is theatrical – high peaks, spectacular gorges, rivers welling up from the underworld, and to the north-west the shapes of unknown mountains in an alien land. In such a setting, it is not only the psychological truth of Greek myths which is borne in on one; it is their actuality. I felt sometimes on these shoulders of the Pindus, that I was seeing one landscape, but sensing another stranger one; that I was standing on one kingdom with its rivers all round me, but was very aware that below its surface lay another place, with other rivers, an unfished underworld where myth and actuality blended and became one truth.

I made two trips in succeeding years to the Voithamatis and on the first of these, having limited time, decided to concentrate on the water for a couple of miles above and below the bridge on the Konitsa road. It looked most attractive water, with full, cold streams of great clarity. White pebbles and peach-coloured boulders give one the impression that there was nothing in the river, for such water would have no place for fish to conceal themselves. I have had the same feeling often on the Aberdeenshire Dee and have thought I could see every stone in a thin stream when a salmon has materialised and taken my fly. On the Voithamatis, however, under a glittering Greek July sky, this clarity and whiteness daunted me at first. It was stunning to look at, but it made the approach to the waterside, let alone the fish, extremely difficult. Fish were sometimes painfully visible in the streams. As I fished, however, I re-discovered the rule that it is often the fish you don't see which you take. You can give yourself tunnel vision staring at a fish in these conditions. Focusing on one trout hovering on the fin in its clear glide, you can fail to see another nearby and it can be this other fish which takes your fly. Interestingly too, I relearned a lesson there which I had first been given as a boy in Scotland; that water can be its own cover – that a stream can hide you from the fish if you keep low as you wade in, even if, from a high bank, you can see down into it as if it were glass.

I fished my way up to where an old Turkish pack bridge crosses the river about a kilometre up from the road. It was a high arched structure of tremendous grace. Here a flood barrier had been thrown across the river in the shape of a weir with a little fish ladder set into it and a complex of races below. In these streams below the weir (which was showing signs of breaking up when I was there) I found some of the best trout of the visit. The trout were half-a-pound or thereabouts, often smaller, but the annoying thing was that at regular intervals, it was whitefish which took the dry fly. These fish were much freer rising than the trout and I had the impression that they were preventing me from getting to the better trout. The whitefish were terrible wetters of the dry fly. In Scotland it is parr and small trout we swear at as wetters; in Canada it was small fish called shiners. I do not know the Greek for 'wetters' but I know the adjectives I would have added to the noun, because they nearly ruined my sport there. Above the weir, near the pack bridge, however, there were no whitefish to be seen. I followed the river up, raising a trout here and there and was soon raising, landing and returning fish of four to eight ounces. I soon found that it was impossible to go on upstream and reach the limestone gorges where I was sure the best of the pools would be. I was forced back on both banks and had to content myself on that first visit with the access-ible, and not very productive water above and below the road bridge. But I had, at least, found catchable trout in Greece.

I was returning that evening from the river and I stopped for some-thing to eat in a very small taverna somewhere on the Konitsa road and there I had a wine which I think was called Zitsa. It was a white fairly lightly resinated retsina made by the champagne method, that is made effervescent in the bottle. It was excellent and although I asked for it in many other places in Greece, I never found it again. In the taverna I asked about trout and was assured that in the Voithamatis were trout of large size, 'several kilos in weight'. During my first short visit to the river, however, I saw nothing of them and thought I should perhaps treat the taverna stories as merely encouraging myth. That first visit was short and exploratory and it was almost a year later, the following July, when I had the opportunity to return to the area for a week. At the local checkpoint the police guard was interested. He told me he knew of heavy trout in the middle Voithamatis, but not in the section

I had fished the previous year. How could I get there? Ah, there was a road, little known and very rough. He came out and looked at my car and said, as a Gaelic ghillie might have said: 'Well... maybe.... You *might* be all right.'

I was to find out what he meant. He showed me the place where the track turned off the main road and I found I was able to pick my way along it, uncomfortably, but reasonably well. The track struck off east towards the mountains and several times looked like tracks which I have tried to drive elsewhere in Greece and Crete where roads become tracks, then ruts through the trees, then goat paths from which one has to reverse out, defeated. This track, however, wound on and some twelve miles up into the hills, eventually reached the villages of Aristi and Panigon. It reached the Voithamatis in a lovely glade at the bottom of a steep twisting hill. This was the much talked about middle section. Here, below Aristi, I crossed the river by a temporary bridge and entered a lovely wooded valley between an upstream and a downstream gorge, both, I thought, impenetrable. This is the stretch once reserved for Queen Frederika of Greece. A plaque on a rock near the bridge recalls her fishing there. This lovely section of river was full of trout, many of them highly visible from the bridge or any high bank. Trout would sidle away from you as you walked by the water. I edged upstream in that glittering clear river and had the frustration of seeing trout after trout gliding away from me before I could do as much as raise my rod, let alone present a dry fly.

There was not much surface activity by day on the deep pools and limestone glides, but trout did pop up here and there in the strong light. Sometimes you found that you were trying a fly over a fish you could see clearly. I remembered my first experience of an English chalk stream, the Wylye in Wiltshire, when I was a young RAF recruit being trained at Yatesbury. I was used to clear rivers in Scotland, but not so clear that you could see the spots on the fish as they hung in the glides. If the Wylie was clear, the Voithamatis was unbelievable crystal. Yet, by careful wading and waiting like a statue ready to cast, I did take trout that first afternoon. I raised and missed several on the dry fly, and eventually hooked only two small fish. Then I changed to upstream nymph and tying on a fine, long leader of light nylon, and casting a long and careful line, I explored the water. I had two quick rises, small fish which I returned. Then I took a half-pounder, and felt things were improving. Sometimes I had periods of moving fish and failing to contact them, but at other times I found the takes, even in the bright Greek sun, sincere and solid.

The fish I was contacting were all smallish, not above half-a-pound, but they were great fun and the place was so spectacular. I was, like the upstream fishers of the Borders near my home, both a fisher and a traveller. I fished and worked my way upstream, exploring runs, walking past pools like green wells, occasionally seeing shadowy large trout in inaccessible potholes. As I went I found the gorge becoming difficult. I had to cling to difficult paths to get upstream and I was aware that some of the going was more suited to someone in climbing boots than waders. I wanted to press on, however, because I had met before I left Athens a group of Canadian geologists who were working in the Pindus and one of them told me that the Voithamatis at one point in its upper gorge doubled its flow where a vast surge of water welled up out of a great sink hole. I wanted very much to see that. It would be like the very entrance to the underworld. I pushed on up a bank which was growing more and more steep and dangerous. On my right, the river began to show very deep pools lying in pots dissolved from the rock, some of immense depth. Looking down from some of the vertiginous paths I was clinging to I saw one or two trout which took my breath away – trout which looked like salmon, finning in the clear water on the lips of dark green holes into which, when they detected my approach, they quietly sank. Some of these fish must have been four or five pounds in weight. But they were untouchable trout, in unapproachable pools. Short of an inflatable boat, I could not think of a way to cover them with a fly. I wondered if the hole would be like that, dark green and with shadowy large trout on its lip, trout from the other world. But the path became impossible, and time was passing. Reluctantly, I turned back, leaving the entry to the underworld undiscovered.

The sun each afternoon left the gorge early and the high sides brought a strange chill to the water and cast weird shadows. The first day this happened as I searched for the sink hole, I found it menacing and I moved downstream a little anxiously as the light slanted over the gorge and the deformed shadows grew. Downstream, in the wooded glade, I returned to a more welcoming world. The glides were alive now with rising trout. It was marvellous to see. The light was weaker and the mountain air had lost its afternoon harshness and had become gentle, with even a hint of moisture in it. I watched the rises, and I saw at first what seemed to be an olive riding down, then a large black gnat. I tied on a black dry fly, but only succeeded in raising fish without a touch. This happened several times, then, in frustration, I changed my cast where I stood in the river, thigh deep, and put on two nymphs, as if I were trouting in the Tweed. A trout arched over the cast at once and I had him. Half a pound. I had another, again a spectacular take. Why would the fish not take my dry fly when the surface was pocked with their rises? The answer was, I think, that the rises were not to the surface at all. They were to the nymphs stuck in the surface film. As soon as this penny dropped I decided to wade gently downstream, casting my two small wet flies out on a long line over the glides near the trees and as I did so my bag began to mount. I took four, then six, then ten, twelve and finally sixteen, all of which I returned except a brace of fish to be grilled for supper. It was a wonderful piece of activity that first evening. The best fish was over three-quarters of a pound and when I hooked it I was sure I was into one of the policeman's monsters. All the trout were beautifully marked, were very lively and were delicious to eat...

I returned four times on that trip to fish this wooded region between the two gorges near Aristi. The trout in there behaved more like Scottish fish than the big ones of the gorges, which were like the most educated chalk stream fish in their behaviour. The wooded middle section of the river had patches of brownish weed, which the gorges did not show. The best trout were all below these dark patches. My catches over the four days I spent on my second trip to the Voithamatis were, I think, representative of the stock. There were plenty of trout averaging half a pound with a scattering of heavier fish. In the four days I fished this section, why did I not once hook a policeman's trout of a kilo or two? I had seen fish of this quality in the pools, but they were either unapproachable or were not interested in my flies. Going over his story in my mind, I wonder if there is a kind of hidden message in it, between the lines. I think he was telling me that, after Queen Frederika's day, locals blasted the river again? Then the military restrictions came in 1967 and that ushered in a period of recovery for the rivers of the area. I fished the river in 1970 and 1971 and I was conscious of a generation gap in the trout I saw. There were plenty of juveniles and a few grandfathers, but not much between. The river was re-stocking itself. The population gap is almost a political and a conservation commentary. Without total control, Greek waters often suffer from a free-for-all blast-them-out anarchy. Only when restrictions can be enforced, as, for example, in a military zone, can a river recover.

The uniqueness of the Voithamatis environment is confirmed by fishing neighbouring Pindus rivers. The nearby Aoos to the north is a lovely river in many ways but where the Voithamatis is white and peach, the Aoos is black since its waters flow over dark, sometimes black sand. There, after some hard walking and fishing up into the valley, I finally gave up after taking nothing but whitefish. It seems that wherever whitefish have appeared, they have taken over, much as grayling have done in some British waters. I had the same experience in other Pindus rivers. Fishing down through the Epirus, and sampling waters as I went, I came across headwaters which held good trout, but lower river reaches where the whitefish had taken over completely. There are good trout up to about a pound and a half in the headwaters of the Arachthos (including the high Metsovon river). One of my

Canadian geologist friends, who spent many weeks out on the remotest parts of the Pindus, reported that he had taken many good trout on his small spinning rod as he explored, but he also reported that, even in the remotest regions of the mountains, fish trapping and blasting in past years had ruined rivers near villages.

I worked my way south and fished small and large rivers as I crossed them, walking some way into the mountains here and there to sample the fishing available. I fished the Louros, for example, a very green river with opaque water, whose banks were often marshy and froggy and in some places there I almost trod on snakes. The trout there were solid pounders and better, but were thinly spread. Here again there were whitefish and chub and catfish, all competing for fly or bait, although I never took a catfish on the fly myself. If you are travelling in this region, by the way, don't be misled by tavernas which advertise fresh local trout grilled over charcoal. These fish are farmed rainbows and, in my view, are not worth cooking compared with wild trout.

The search for Greek trout took me to some of the loveliest places in the country. The fish were memorable, but I do not remember the Pindus rivers because of the weight and numbers of fish taken. It was absolutely not a fishmongering journey; it was a special experience. It took me to regions of Greece seldom visited, to spectacular river scenery in the heart of mountains sung about by Homer and the poets. It was memorable, moving landscape. It was, when I was there, unspoiled, at least temporarily. Perhaps it was a privileged time to be allowed to fish there, to sample a Greece which elsewhere has disappeared. That marvellous landscape possesses me. But it is not the sculpted rocks alone which have impressed me most; it is the atmosphere of the gorges which lingers and haunts me – the indescribable feeling of fishing waters of the underworld which emerge from their timeless, shaded springs to flow through time and foster trout for a mile or two.

CHAPTER
12

The taimen of Inari

THE NORTHERN TERRITORIES of Finnish Lapland are dominated by
Lake Inari, which lies like a great island–studded sea north of the
villages of Ivalo and Inari and covers virtually the whole nothern extent
of that part of Lapland lying between three hundred and four hundred
miles north of the Arctic circle. Only a narrow corridor of Norwegian
Finnmark separates Finland in this northern tundra from the shores
of the Arctic Sea. On the east, Russia begins at a point almost
touching Lake Inari and runs over the Kola peninsula and the White Sea
to its huge landmass reaching back to the Urals and Siberia beyond.
Inari is the focus of the northern–flowing rivers of that part of Lapland
and principal among these is the Juutuanjoki. The first picture I ever
saw of Lapland was of the then new tourist inn at Inari sitting on the
banks of a streamy wide reach of the Juutuanjoki. It could have been
the best of the Dee in Scotland magnified by a factor of three. That
picture, seen when I was a student, glowed with an almost mystical
power and drew me to make the first of my numerous visits to Finnish
Lapland.

What the picture did not show was what fish the river held. My
mind does not abhor that kind of vacuum. It embraces it, and fills it.
I peopled that river with fish from my own mind. It looked like a
salmon river, so I imagined salmon in it. It looked like an amazing trout
stream, so I imagined it to be full of two–pounders. But I was to
discover that the Juutuanjoki was quite different. It certainly had its
good trout and grayling streams, but it had no salmon, and may never
have had any. It had however in its great streams and pools a remarkable fish which I have met nowhere else but in Finnish Lapland, the

taimen, a very large trout of salmon size. When I looked in admiration and longing at the first pictures of the Juutuanjoki, my imagination quite simply failed to construct such a fish, for the simple reason that a *taimen* was beyond my ken. Now that I have met it, however, the *taimen* haunts me, as it does other anglers who have had the fortune to discover it and it has become, for me, one of the powerful symbols of the rare and disappearing Finnish wilderness. That symbol, however, has now slipped deeper into my mind. The mysterious and rare *taimen* has become the ultimate trout and I feel immensely privileged that I was once or twice allowed to contact it – no, the word is too weak; I was allowed to wrestle with it, as a kind of dark but dazzling angel.

Lake Inari drains north east and reaches the Arctic via the river the Russians call the Paatsi, but which Finns call the Petsamo and which for part of its route forms the frontier between USSR and Norway's Finnmark. Lake Inari tentatively reaches out an eastern arm, as a cat might advance a paw, to touch Russia, but, apart from that overture, it draws back from the Russian frontier and locates itself firmly in Finland. The Petsamo, which drains the lake, was Finnish until the end of the Second World War, when the land round it was ceded to Russia. It was a salmon water and there are accounts of at least one British angler fishing this water for salmon in the 1930s (Halliday Sutherland: *Lapland Journey*). Whether salmon from the Arctic ever reached Lake Inari in the past, or whether obstacles, natural and artificial prevented them from running the whole way, I do not know. When I asked about this during my planning to fish in the area and when I made my first trips to Inari, I was slightly thrown by constant references to *lohi*, which means 'salmon'. I was also told of *lohi* of over twenty pounds and was shown flies which had taken these fish – all large single-hooked salmon flies, 6/0 and 8/0, fully dressed Jock Scotts or Black Doctors, looking as if they had been selected from Hardy's catalogue for 1910. I was also shown a rod in Inari which was used for these fish and it turned out to be a Hardy sixteen-foot salmon fly rod with a steel centre. The stories of 'salmon' in Inari and particularly in the Juutuanjoki River eventually turned out to be stories about the *taimen*, which are not salmon at all in the common sense. These fish are great trout. They are spoken about with some reverence all over Finland, but the best stories, and the best surviving *taimen*, are in Lapland. The *taimen* of Inari have the reputation of being the largest in Finland and they form a migratory population of fish of salmon size, using Lake Inari as their feeding grounds and the Juutuanjoki and other tributaries of the lake as their spawning streams. In the late summer and autumn they run from the lake and are taken in the rapids and pools of the Juutuanjoki. For me, they are the great charismatic fish of Lapland. When I first saw that picture of the inn by the wide streams of an unknown river and was gripped by it, I must have sensed that trout of leviathan size ran its streams. That picture changed me. I had populated its streams as I gazed on it with fish from my own imagination, and they were all puny beside the *taimen*. My imagined trout were also all much more catchable than the *taimen*. In my visits to Inari, I did catch *taimen*, in the Juutuanjoki and elsewhere, but these catches were not common occurrences. I caught them, but I also lost them, heard about them, discussed them and longed for them. I was taken to see one huge fish, lying in state on a stone slab, as one might be taken to see the body of a dead emperor. I look back now on the *taimen* of Inari as one might look back on childhood mountains. They loomed over one and exerted a power over one far in excess of their number or size. I still feel the power of these magnificent fish. I still have branded in my mind the first pull from one and the first sight of a great spotted flank arching through a fast stream of the Juutuanjoki. In the river which runs through the psyche of every angler there must be a place for *taimen*, for a secretive, longed for run of trout of astonishing quality, for fish celebrated in folklore, misnamed, lied about, occasionally caught, admired and recalled in awe by those who had the good chance to fall under their influence.

The fishing on the Juutuanjoki centres on its rapids. While there are long glides and streams and fine gentle pools on the river where I dis-covered good grayling and some trout temptable with a dry fly, the rapids, where the river roared down over rocks and formed fat streams and pools, concentrated the fishing water in a series of holding pools and streams as a Scottish salmon river would also do. In the ten miles or so of the Juutuanjoki immediately above Inari there are three sets of rapids, all reachable by a forest road and fishable. On my first day on the river, I walked up to the first of these rapids, Janiskoski, set up my ten-foot fly rod, selected a couple of sea trout flies and an eight-pound cast and fished down a stream. I had several decent trout and grayling within half-an-hour. Above me the main rapid of Janiskoski poured down in noisy white water. A wooden cord road, for portaging boats round the white water, led me further up to a rocky section where the river gathered itself before pouring down into the white turbulence below. It was a difficult river to get into. Most of the streams were formidable and were both unwadeable and unboatable. As it happened, I had no boat. I therefore looked for eddies and sheltered spots on the sides of the most apprachable streams and I began fishing them down, wading as well as I could with thigh boots and casting a long line.

I was searching out a deep flank to a fast stream, where glassy water signalled lies, when I had a strong swirl to the cast and a pull like a salmon and I was into something powerful which turned and ran immediately out into the hard water of the rapid and, in the middle of rushing water, rose in a great cartwheel and gave me a split second's glimpse of a marvellous trout with gold and olive and white showing and spots like sixpences. It was salmon size, but fought quite differently. There was a doggedness and determination which the salmon lacks. That fish hammered through the fast water with a great throbbing rush which alarmed me. How would I ever hold it in the rapids? It would drown my line, leap again and that would be that. The fish, however, turned and ran back towards the apron of the stream where it had been hooked, as if the rapids beyond were hostile to it. I recovered line and found that, although I had several more runs to cope with, the trout did not want to face the heavy white current of the outer streams again. It did fight deeply however and it pulled my cast round several nasty boulders in the water not far below me. I had two flies on, in Scottish sea trout style, Mallard and Claret size eight and a Soldier Palmer on the dropper. When I felt the rocks touching the cast, I wished I had used only one. There was an imminent danger of snagging the dropper and losing the fish. Then it happened. I felt the snag, then the pluck which suggested a broken dropper and I waited for the parting of the cast. It did not come. The contact seemed as sound as ever, but I was wary of my cast. I fought the fish in to the side and found that it kept its head down into the depths and began to circle and tug in a dour way, tired, but difficult to bring to the top. I saw the line emerging, then the knot at the top of the nine-foot cast, then the knot one yard further down where the dropper should have been and only a blood knot remained. I tried to be gentle. I know how unreliable a blood knot can be when a dropper is broken off. I had still to see the fish, except for that memorable glimpse as it showed in its first great run. Then I saw it, a dark back below the glassy surface of the stream. It turned again and made a weak circle and I unhitched my net and worked the trout round once more. I know you shouldn't net a fish until it is lying on its side on the surface, safe and still. I was not happy about my cast, however, and was desperate not to lose this trout, which was bigger than any trout I had ever hooked at that time. When the fish circled again, I knew it was only just below the surface and I put the net in, moved the fish round towards it and in a sense groped with the net for it, dangerously, and felt great relief when I got the fish into the bag of the net on the first try. I lifted it out and went ashore and laid the fish in the net on the moss well back from the edge. I looked at it. It was a wonderful fish. I had never seen such a trout before, and I have not seen many since. It was like a fat half-pounder scaled up. The head was small, the shoulder rose like the fattest of sea trout, the girth was outstanding for the length, giving all the signals of a fish stuffed with food and in perfect condition. The flanks were strewn with scores of squarish black and dark grey spots which were also scattered over the gill covers to the eye. The general colour of the flanks was golden, shading to an olive brown back, also heavily spotted. It was a *taimen*, six pounds in weight, by no means large by the standards of the water, but a wonderful fish to take on the kind of tackle I might have used for Scottish sea trout. It outclassed a salmon of the same size in its fight, and equalled in strength the best fresh sea trout hooked in the same conditions. It had taken a Mallard and Claret on the tail of the cast. I ran my fingers up and found the blood knot where the dropper should have been, tugged it, and it held. I tugged it again, and it gave way. Blood knots with broken droppers fail and I had been within close sight of failure in taking this best trout of my life. If I had lost the dropper before the hard rushes into the outer streams of the rapid, I would have been broken. I was lucky in that I lost my top fly when the fish was tired and was only able to make its last circles in comparatively easy conditions. Fearing a break, I had acted gingerly in the end and had taken the first opportunity to net the fish out. One second's revival, one surface thrashing pull at the net and I would, I believe, have lost the fish. Taking it in these circumstances, with disaster facing me all the time, has made the catch sweeter, as if the fish had been not only tempted and caught but also drawn with luck and possibly a touch of gentleness from a river which would have willingly reclaimed it. I think I was more excited by that fish than I have been with any other since. It had been so long expected and my imagination had been so stoked by the stories, half-truths and fictions about the *taimen* which I had heard since coming to Lapland, that you might have expected the encounter with the fish itself to be an anticlimax. But it was not. It seemed to me to be a triumph. It had also been taken in fairly public water near a tourist inn, wading, and with tackle which the people in the inn thought too light. I came across advice to use heavy tackle quite often in Lapland. There is something in it. It is true that big grayling can smash a light cast of wet flies. It is true also that *taimen* of any size – and they can be three or four times larger than the one I caught that day on the Juutuanjoki – can be formidably strong, but eight-pound stuff and size eight flies are not light tackle! Yet on a single-handed fly rod and size eight flies, I felt closer to trout fishing than salmon fishing in my approach. With this kind of tackle, I have taken many good Scottish sea trout – the largest ten pounds – and I have no real difficulty in bringing in salmon in the teens of pounds on single-handed rods and similar flies and nylon. Yet, even with heavy fish, the single-handed rod gives an intimacy and gentleness in the fishing which can be absent from double-handed rods and would definitely be absent from a Hardy steel-centred sixteen-footer.

I found out that the authorities passed a rule the following year which forbade fishing with flies smaller than size six. It was a zany rule with not much clear thinking behind it. I was told that it was to protect

growing stocks of fish. But I was also told that the rule was something
to do with Lapp politics, in essence keeping the stocks of grayling and
smaller trout for netting. But netting in what is designated a 'sport
river'? I could not fathom this insistence on fishing only large flies for
small fish. This rule effectively stopped dry fly fishing for grayling and
also stopped ordinary wet fly fishing for trout of the one- to two-pound
class. It was a rule which at first was broken by almost every angler
I met on the river. They all said it was ludicrous. Where anglers con-
scientiously kept the rule, fishing was difficult if the quarry was
anything except the larger trout.

A curious result of this rule does not concern *taimen* at all, but
grayling which abound in the rivers of Lapland. I encountered on the
Juutuanjoki an American desperate to catch a two-pound grayling. Fish
were rising within reach, but following the rules, he was quite unable
to make a size six fly float for any length of time and quite unable to
make grayling rise to it. He was sitting disconsolately by a stream on
the river about five miles above Inari. I sympathised with him and said
that by chance I had some small size six dry flies in my box.

'Small size sixes?' he said incredulously.

'Yes. These are special flies', I said, 'They're on specially small size
six hooks, tied in Scotland.'

I produced a size ten, or was it a twelve, Grey Duster, tied it on to
the American's line, cast it out to see if it would float and immediately
rose and hooked a grayling. I gave him the rod and he played the fish
and netted it. It was a two-pound grayling, exactly what he had
dreamed about catching in Lapland. He fished on, and took two more
good fish before I had to go on upstream. He was shaking with
pleasure because of his success, and fished the day out with what he was
prepared to believe was a size six, within the rules of the river. He
departed for home the next day and he left a very happy man. I think
of that incident sometimes as the ideal example of the therapeutic lie. It
was also, on his part, the most willing suspension of disbelief.

There are three rapids of note within ten miles of the inn at Inari. In
my first year I concentrated on exploring the one nearest. I walked and
fished and waded. On one of these days, walking above Janiskoski,
where I had caught my first *taimen*. I discovered a long glide with
islands of rock in it and I found that I could use my thigh waders to
good effect not only to approach the river through a marshy reach but
also to pick out a wading route to one of the rocks and fish a basin
below. I fished wet flies again, but this time in gentler streams. I had
grayling immediately and then some quite reasonable trout. As I fished
on, enjoying this little patch of sport, I hooked a rather small grayling,
perhaps half a pound in weight. It splattered and twirled as I drew it in
and, quite suddenly, a most massive fish appeared and snatched it off

the cast. I was absolutely astonished. It was an enormous trout and seeing it overwhelmed me with a mixture of excitement and terror. I had looked eyeball to eyeball into the face of a trout which seemed capable of opening its mouth and swallowing me! This was Leviathan! It made my hair stand on end. I retreated to a large rock and then to the shore and thought about it. How could such a fish be caught? I had only a ten-foot cane fly rod. I decided that the most intelligent way to catch the fish was to attempt to repeat the incident, so I caught a couple of small grayling in a side stream and mounted one of them with a treble hook at its tail and another at its head, as I might have baited up for pike. I used the heaviest nylon in my bag which I think may have been eight- or nine-pound stuff. I waded in again and lobbed this dead bait out over the basin where Leviathan lay. It wobbled round once and nothing came to it. I tried again and this time he had it. I am not an expert bait fisher. Had I been I would have known better how to set the hooks. As it was, I gave the fish time to turn as if it were a salmon. Then I tightened. Excitement may have lent me just too much haste, but I hooked the fish and was into a massive, strong creature which pulled back into the pot then ran towards me. I shortened on it and it came to the top and I saw that it was a trout of possibly twelve pounds – something like twice the size of the one I had taken the previous day. Heaven knows what it weighed. It seemed colossal anyway. It came up to the top, opened its mouth and turned away as if angered by the hooks, which appeared to be set in the front of its mouth. As it turned, it shook like a dog and sent my dead bait flying out of its mouth and disappeared. It was tragic. I had lost a trout probably bigger than the average Scottish salmon. It was a fascinating encounter, typical of the backwoods of Lapland. I had resorted to a not very refined technique to hook the fish, which I feel right in saying would not have been very interested in a normal trout fly. What a fish! It was a ferocious, cannibal creature, no doubt fat on its predations of the char and shrimp and small trout of Inari. If my first *taimen* had spots like peas on its sides, this one seemed to have spots like plums. I don't think I am exaggerating, even if all the temptations are there to do so. What is absolutely true is that I have never, before or since, moved a trout of this calibre. Those who have had this special kind of angling experience will no doubt agree with me that events like this mix in one both pleasure and a kind of fear. For me they are well set in the wilderness fishings of Lapland.

After one of my days on the Juutuanjoki in the third summer I fished it, when I was using Inari as a staging post for an exploration to waters to the north of the Lake, I arrived back at the inn to hear that a large *taimen* had been taken by fly in the river the previous night. It was August and the nights in Lapland actually had an hour or two of darkness, or deep gloom. It had been taken from a boat on a harled salmon fly. I asked to see it and I was led through buildings at the back of the inn to a storehouse with a concrete floor and there, lying in state, with a strange air of silence round it was a marvellously thick, well-conditioned fish. It was bigger in girth and shoulder than a salmon. Indeed, only the best sea trout could have matched it for shape and depth. It was greyish in appearance, and had none of the colours my smaller fish had shown. It had been out of the water for some hours before I saw it, of course, and colour fades.

'What a marvellous *taimen*,' I said, 'Well done. What does it weigh?'

'Six kilos', the captor said. 'It's the biggest so far this year.'

I reflected that six kilos was over fourteen pounds. The fish had, however, none of the nastiness of form we sometimes find in a *ferox* – the big head, the ugly jaw, signs of a fish going back, rapacious and sour. It looked like a well-conditioned sea trout scaled up. It was magnificent.

'Would you like to hold it?' my friend asked.

'Yes, I would.'

I lifted the fish up by the gills, and felt its dead weight. It was a fish like the large one I had lost in a previous summer on the same river. As a dead weight that *taimen* was impressive enough, but resurrected and hooked in fast water at night it would have been formidable. The largest fish of this sort I heard reliably referred to weighed twelve kilograms (26.4 pounds) and was taken in the Juutuanjoki. It must have fought like an armed torpedo hooked at night from a narrow boat! These fish so far outclass other trout in Lapland that it is not surprising that they have become legends. Unfortunately, another reason for their becoming legends is that they are scarce. Lake Inari, however, is like an inland sea and there they have some degree of safety and an excellent food supply. They have char, grayling, perch and pike fry and a plentiful supply of shrimps. I was to learn from experiences elsewhere, that large trout in Lapland are omniverous, taking a range of food which we might have thought was more typical of pike.

The *taimen* in its heavier weights becomes a rather specialised fish for the angler. It is fished at night, with heavy tackle, large flies and in special places at special times. I think I compromised when I was fishing for them, trying to keep them in the category 'trout', when the locals in Inari all kept referring to them as 'salmon'. It may sound Irish, but I was probably lucky to take only a six-pounder on my first day of the first year I fished that marvellous river. A ten- or fifteen-pounder might have done two things; it would have broken me and would have convinced me that I should lay aside the single-handed rod and harl large salmon flies at night. My inclination is to fish a single-handed rod with castable flies and take my *taimen* as they come. The years I spent fishing for them in the Juutuanjoki and on other rivers in Lapland brought me numerous fish in the three- and four-pound class in forest streams where these fish were marvellous captures. I have really shunned the 'light engineering' approaches taken by the dedicated Leviathan fishers. This is just my nature. I am a kind of hedonist. In fishing terms this means maximising the pleasure I get from certain types of fishing, for example, from casting a fly on a single-handed rod for trout and sea trout, rather than taking up the bait rod, or harling uncastable flies and plugs behind a boat. This is where I slightly part company with my colleagues who become obsessed, as opposed to inspired, by *taimen*. I want to walk in the forest and explore streams and wade as I fish. I think I have an explorer's sense of trout, including *taimen*, rather than a specialist's view. Many Finns would say I was just a *tammukka* fisher – that is, a fisher for small trout. This is an important distinction in Finland. If trout are small and have red spots as well as black they are *tammukka* and if they have only black spots they are *lohi* or *taimen*. The absence of red spots is, for some addicts, the sign of success and it can produce anomalies. I was once in a narrow Lapp boat going up the Lemmenjoki, a tributary of the Juutuanjoki, and a Finnish angler was trolling a devon behind the boat as we slowly motored over a lake en route. He had a take from a trout about a pound-and-a-half in size. He swung the fish in and looked at it. It was silvery and had no red spots. When he saw this, he lifted his head and in a great voice which made the wilderness ring he shouted: 'Lohi!'

Lightning had struck. It was the moment of great consummation. It would have been churlish to point out that the fish was little more than frying-pan size and would have been a nice take on the dry fly with a two-pound leader, red spots or no red spots. In matters of principle and deep emotion like this, these arguments are irrelevant. I should perhaps say no more, however, lest I hold up a mirror to my own nature and see my own eccentricities and anomalies as an angler. I suppose I rejoice more over a fresh two-pound sea trout than I do over a three- or four-pound brown trout when the fish are taken on fly at night. I delight more over a salmon which shows as it takes a small fly fished on a floating line, than I do over a salmon of twice the size which pulls my sunk fly deep down. Peculiarities and addictions abound in fishing and it is really rather inconsistent that it is only the other man's cult which seems slightly ridiculous. My years of looking for *taimen*, being inspired by them and occasionally catching them have thrilled me. But I long to catch them on my trout rod, like a lucky *tammukka* fisher, and that is largely how it has happened to me. I'm prejudiced too, of course, and want the rod to bend hard into a great trout. But when I see the red spots on a two- or three-pounder, they are 'rose stipples

upon trout that swim' and not the sign that, yet again, the extraordinary *taimen* has eluded me.

I found *taimen* in several other waters of Finland and Lapland, but
they have always remained an exotic, almost unreal fish for me. What
I think of when I look back on my several summers in the far north of
Finland is a most gripping natural landscape of old trees, multitudinous
lakes and streams and rivers and a range of fish – trout, grayling, char,
whitefish, and others – scattered throughout. Like Scotland, Lapland
rises from its tree-lined river vallies to fells where burns and lochs run
through expansive regions of boulders, rock and moss. On the higher
hills, snow lies until July. Sometimes fish would be found in plenty;
sometimes we searched for them in clear, apparently empty and infertile
waters. My journeys in various regions of the north have, however, left
me with a rich array of experiences, some unique and others reinforcing
the deepest feelings I had from my own Scottish trout and salmon
fishing. The settings of the fishing and the wilderness journeys I made
in Lapland have taken on the qualities of touchstones; they are fundamental, essential. They took place where fisher and Nature meet eye to
eye. While elements of this are present in all fishing, the starkness and
clarity of the Lapland experience has a way of making one see clearly
the colours which elsewhere are often blurred. That first alluring
picture of the river at Inari started it all, but what I was to find in other
places made the Juutuanjoki, with its roads, its school and its comfortable inn, seem urban.

CHAPTER

13

The forest of Luttojoki

ONLY THE HEADWATERS of the Luttojoki river are in Finland. At Rajojooseppi it crosses the USSR frontier and flows north-east to the White Sea. The headwaters, however, dividing into numerous forest streams, form a marvellous tract of Lapland, all the more fascinating because the Lutto becomes the Russian Lotta and reaches out of our ken, to become one of the northern salmon rivers of the USSR. We had a glimpse of this link with the White Sea the day we arrived. On a long pool where we were pausing to sort out our packs before fording the Luttojoki, I saw a salmon. I was packed and ready to ford the river and had half-an-hour to spare. To redeem the time, I set up a trout rod and cast a fly down the pool below the fording point. I caught nothing, but soon after beginning I saw what was unmistakably a large, thin kelt salmon splashing in the pool. My companion, Jaakko Uotila, explained that it was perfectly possible for a salmon to be there. Although the Russians had built power stations on the Lotta downstream, by agreement, they netted out ascending salmon and released them above the obstructions. One fish, I hope not solitary, had reached these head-waters, had presumably spawned and was now, as an emaciated, weak kelt unlikely to make the long journey back down to the sea. It was August. I have never seen a later kelt, nor felt more the loneliness and lingering death of a spent fish than I did when that thin salmon splashed.

We forded the Luttojoki and struck up one of its tributaries, the Suomojoki, a clear forest river running over gravel and shingle. We fished a little as we went, finding smallish grayling and trout here and there, but our objective was deeper into the forest – a small, extra-ordinary stream with the name Murravarrakkajoki, which for some reason makes the Finns laugh, as Tillietudlum or Auchtermuchty might at home. Although he had never been there before, Jaakko had facts about the Murravarrakkajoki. He spoke about the forest and the deep pools of the stream and lurking, large trout. We talked about it that first night by the Suomojoki as we camped among the trees. Each stirred expectations in the other about a stream neither had seen, as pilgrims might as they rested on the way to a shrine. The banks of the Suomo, along which our route lay, were suited to longings. They were thickly forested as many lower lying rivers are in Lapland, pillared with large old *manty*, tall, red-barked pines with deep green canopies, like our dwindling Caledonian forest in Scotland. Birches clustered in clearings and along the river margins where they could find soil among the rocks. Here and there an aspen would quiver beside a birch. We were in a venerable, living, ancient forest, with columns and tapestries centuries old, like a great abbey. The pines in this Lapland forest mature over great reaches of time, taking centuries to grow to full size. The Luttojoki and Suomojoki forest in which we were travelling is not a forest on its own. It is part of a great tract of old European trees which still reaches from Scotland, through Scandinavia to Finland and, not many miles to the east of Suomojoki, merges with the extensive northern Russian pine forests. We were witnesses of a distinguished piece of living natural history. In this ancient forest, however, side by side with the present living generation of old trees stand impressive dead pines, trees which have grown to slow maturity and died as they stood, to form the *kello*, barkless, seasoned, tall silvery-grey columns, which ring to the back of your axe with reverberating tones as though they had the power to sing. Centuries of life and centuries of death go into that ringing sound. In the long dead *kello*, the forest, in addition to its music, has its own chronicles, and its own relics which, like well understood history, signal continuity and provide perspectives for the living.

We expressed hope and anticipation that night and, later, some longings. I said I longed to see an elk – to part a curtain of birch and see one knee-deep in the river, or to surprise one browsing in a forest clearing. It was possible, Jaakko said, but rare. In that setting, round a camp fire, longings crossed the border of the possible and ranged into myth. I found myself almost hoping for the sight of a unicorn, or for a terrifying glimpse of Leviathan somewhere in the forest streams or lakes. Fishing has much of the stuff of dreams and myth in it. We imagine, we construct and we hope; we people streams and lakes with the products of our own mythologies. Sometimes we delight ourselves with imagined catches – generous discoveries in deep pools. Sometimes we terrify ourselves, letting childish dreams and collective myths combine to produce monsters. It was in this mood we talked that night, then slept and continued in the morning towards our forest stream.

Our first two days were spent walking into the forest, taking it in reasonably easy stages. On the second night, we turned east into the Murravarrakkajoki valley, which we followed some way up and settled for the night in a peaceful clearing where there was access down a steep bank to the stream. We ate our evening meal and prepared to turn in. I picked my way down to the water's edge to wash and I stooped down, cupped water in my hands and splashed it on my face. Then, through my wet eyelids I saw, lying on a flat silvery stone beside the stream, two gold rings. I looked again, hard. Yes, they were there. Gold rings in the middle of Lapland? We were two days out into a deep primal forest. We had camped at that spot because we were tired. I had made my way down the bank, through the birches, making my own random path and had stumbled on two gold rings! I can hardly record my sense of surprise, nor the confused feeling of privilege which accompanied it. I picked the rings up and felt quietened and moved. The strangeness of the find seemed to illuminate them and I began to feel that I had somehow met the rings rather than found them. I had travelled inexorably over miles of fell and forest to a rendezvous. It was as though some voice said, 'Here they are!' when I saw the rings. If I had been searching for them, what an end it would have been to see them through wet eyelids! But it did not feel like an end. Finding the rings felt like part of a strange process, not yet over.

I closed my hand over the rings and climbed the bank to tell Jaakko. 'I've found two wedding rings,' I said.

It must have been the most unexpected of statements from a fishing companion. He didn't believe me.

'They were on a stone in a stream in the river. They were just lying there, waiting to be picked up.'

Jaakko looked at the rings.

'Heavens! They *are* wedding rings. Someone must have lost them.'

'But two?' I asked.

'Women wear one on their right hand when they become engaged and one on their left – or both – when they marry. The simplest explanation is that a woman has washed here recently and taken off her rings and has lost them.'

His explanation was sober, probable, very likely correct. Yet we sat looking at these rings for some time and our feelings were far from scientific. Jaakko's explanation covered only a fraction of the experience of finding the rings. I certainly felt, as I suspect Jaakko did also, that there was an event within an event to come to grips with. We had a coincidence and a mystery on our hands. I felt, too, that the forest and the river were witnesses to the whole story. Indeed, the more I thought, the more I believed that they were also collaborators in a mystery which might never be solved.

The following day, we made our way upstream, fishing streams here and there, feeling our way into a river new to us. We caught small trout and grayling. Nothing spectacular. As we penetrated deeper into the woods, however, the pools became deeper and the glides cut under shady banks and the trout became larger. We found ourselves walking along beside a deep green pool with overhanging tree-clad banks on our third day when we saw dimly in the gentle flow a line of trout like shadows in the water. They were all several pounds in weight. We stopped, had a council of war and I decided to try these marvellous fish with a dry fly. I crept up to them as if they had been chalk stream fish, but not one moved to the fly, I changed my tactics and crept downstream, offering them a wet fly. This time, they did react. They saw the fly and in a leisurely way turned away from it and sidled quietly into the gloom beneath the bank as salmon might when they are disturbed. Jaakko rested them and then tried with a drifted bubble float and a fly, keeping well back from the fish. This merely drove them into hiding. We seemed to to have discovered some marvellous trout, but were they uncatchable?

We decided to set up camp for a few days near this interesting stretch of the Murravarrakkajoki and we found a clear area in the forest with *kello* near a large pool on an S-bend of the river. Below the pool there was a deep run behind fallen timber with the stream biting hard in under the bank. We turned in for the night and decided to spend the whole of the next day trying for trout up and downstream from our camp site. I was up early and I crept down to the deep run near our camp and cast a wet fly down it, keeping my head down behind a fallen tree. I had a take and after a flurry of a fight I netted a large trout of just under three pounds. It was festooned with spots, some of which were red. It was the type of trout the Finns call *tammukka*, that is a stream trout, not a *taimen* which would have large black spots, and would perhaps run up into the stream from a lake where it had fed and grown large. It was not a particularly handsome fish, but had the large head one would associate with a trout which had turned cannibal. That fish had taken the fly, but when I opened it to clean it, I found that its gizzard contained a small mouse. I had never before seen this in a trout. Small fish, insects of all sizes, snails and frogs, yes, but mice, never before. I told Jaakko and his reaction was immediate: 'I think I have the solution to the uncatchable trout we saw yesterday!'

He moved off downstream and I fished on, taking another trout and returning a third in the streamy water near our camp. Jaakko returned an hour later carrying a massive trout of four-and-a-half pounds. It was a superb fish, well-shaped, without the big hungry head my large fish had had and beautifully marked with large black spots grading into a deep brown back:

'What did you catch that on?' I asked

'A mouse!' he said.

He went on to say that he had found in his fishing bag a wobbling plug intended for pike, but which he thought would look like a mouse in the water. The trout thought so too, and he caught this large fish and lost another before the pool became too disturbed.

During the next two or three days we caught fish on flies, and at least one more on a mouse. It was a strange little stream. It seemed to have few small fish. Its population of trout were scattered and were all large. It is likely that the large fish were cannibals and had cleared out the smaller fry, leaving themselves kings of a diminishing food source, and turning to any form of protein they could find, including mice. We had a chance to discuss this with a solitary frontier guard who appeared, rucksack on back, rod in hand. He too had had occasional fish from the deep pools in that river, some well on into the forest, but the big ones were few and far between, he confirmed. We asked him about other anglers and he said there were none further into the woods and anyway the Russian frontier was not far away.

'What does the frontier look like?' I asked.

'It is a reindeer fence', he said.

I thought that was appropriate. I would have been worried to find an Iron Curtain among the pines.

That forest was very conducive to talk. Jaakko and I talked and sang in our camp in that remote and lovely place. I built a small table from bits of pine and we amused ourselves by dining long in the evenings and talking into the night. He was a lecturer in international law, later to become a professor, then Rector in Tampere University. He was a lover of music but he combined with his aesthetic sense a wide practicality, as many Finns do. He loved the woods and was an expert walker, camper and angler. He fascinated me, for example, when he talked about making different kinds of fires. The one we used there was called a *rakkevalkia* and was made of two six-foot long dead pine logs with the fire between. A third log could be set on top and this could keep the fire in indefinitely. Inside the logs, embers always glowed and cooking was simply a matter of opening up the large logs and setting a pan on top. A *rakkevalkia* he said could be used even in the depths of winter for sleeping out without a tent. One man would lie on each side of the logs and would survive the night, whereas a round fire heated only its own small circle.

Using a tin plate I made pancakes on that fire and it was not impossible to discover us eating pancakes and singing as darkness fell. Jaakko was a Sibelius fan and for days kept talking about the tone poem which he called 'Satu' and we merely call 'A Saga'. Jaakko sang all the themes to me in that solitary forest, 'Pum pa-pum, Pum pa-pum, pa-da da da da da pum pa-pum'. I have never forgotten these atmospheric enunciations of the themes of the piece. It might have been Sibelius himself drawing the tunes out of the forest. I had less to offer. I sang Schubert's 'Trout' and Jaakko in a great cascade of pahs and dahs did wonders in evoking the broken chords of the piano accompaniment.

It was a wonderful camp, lacking only the sight of an elk to make it immortal. I did find nearby, however, a single cast antler of an elk, a wonderful evocative giant's hand of bone giving some idea of the size of the creature. It was too heavy to carry. I left it among the trees for the next elk-longing angler to find.

We were sitting at that campfire one evening in silence, eating pancakes when I heard a woman's voice saying 'No!'. It was a very English voice and at first I thought I had produced the sound from my own imagination, or had mistaken the call of a predatory bird. Then it came again, 'No! No!' it said in what seemed peevishness.

Jaako and I stood up. Out of the forest from the eastern side of our camp came an English woman carrying a large rucksack and some paces behind her a Finnish man followed. The woman seemed to be in something of a bad temper. Not only her intonation, but her bearing announced this. She seemed surprised to see us. We greeted her and her companion and invited them to sit down and have a coffee and a pancake. She relaxed a bit but I noticed her companion sitting a little back from her as if this was her party. She poured out her story. She had been walking in the woods for some days with her companion and everything seemed to have gone wrong.

'What do you mean, "gone wrong"?' I asked.

'Oh just everything. And I've lost things.'

'What have you lost', I asked, expecting her to talk about a knife or a cup.

'I've lost my wedding rings', she said.

I could feel my heart beating, but I made myself say, 'That's terrible! Where did you lose them?'

'It must have been somewhere I was washing,' she said, 'but I don't know exactly where.'

I could hold back no longer. I went to my rucksack and pulled out my wallet, opened it and produced the rings.

'Are these the rings?'

She coloured and took them from my hand, then looked at me and said quite quietly, 'Yes.' Then after a pause still looking at the rings said: 'This is a miracle.'

'I found them on a stone a day's walking downstream from here near the junction of this river and the Suomojoki.'

I cannot recall exactly what was said after that. There were long words of gratitude, reams about the coincidence of finding rings on a stone in a river in a forest and she produced a card with her name and an address in London. She said something about her husband being Finnish, but she quickly said that her travelling companion was only a friend. It was a very flushed, bewildered conversation, full of words like 'Amazing,' and 'Miraculous'. Then, rising, she said, 'They *are* my rings. I'm not deluding you!'.

I said I didn't think she was. But she was tense, expecting to be blamed. In this mood, she shook hands with me, put on her rucksack and left with her companion following, heading downstream.

We fished on for two more days, but each of us was becoming aware that we now knew, almost to the individual, all the fish which made up the trout resources of that little stream. We also knew that there were few small fish to grade the gap between the multi-pound fish we had spotted and the small stock of fingerlings. The trout in the Murravarra-kkajoki were strangely like the forest – old, slow-growing, vulnerable and almost irreplaceable. We had taken four, two of which Jaakko had pressed into the bottom of a plastic bucket with salt and dill to take home. We killed no more. The taking of trout like that was not much different from felling an ancient pine tree. Both of us felt it strongly.

We left that extraordinary little river and fished instead on the Suomojoki below, catching small- to middle-sized grayling in a river with more plentiful stock. The day before we left for the Luttojoki and home, we had a clear hot day and we found a treeless hill in the forest, a *tunturi*. There we discovered a great bed of blueberries. Jaakko took a side of *gravadlax* trout out of his fish bucket and we sat on the hill eating trout and blueberries, looking over the treetops of the forest. The beauty and the grace of these old pines was moving. They were comunicating an air of stability, overlapping centuries and making our span of life seem tiny. Rivers threaded the forest and they too communicated their most ancient story, written on the rocks over ages which make the span of the trees seem small. The rocks themselves far pre-date the rivers. On a hill on that pre-Cambrian shield, on the oldest rocks on the globe, I had a deep feeling of my own fragility and transience. Rock-time, river-time and forest-time reduced me to the smallest footnote of existence. Only trout were written in a shorter sentence.

When we got back to the Luttojoki and forded the river we met a small party of anglers on the bank. We asked them how their sport was and one 'glowingly announced that his friend the previous night had caught a salmon, and he indicated the pool.

'Was it a big one?' I asked.

'Yes, very big, but quite thin. He has salted it down to take home for the winter.'

Should I have said, 'It was a miserable kelt!'? I didn't. At least I didn't say it to those who had caught it. I said it later to Jaakko. I felt upset.

I lamented that kelt's death. I had identified with that lone salmon, scores of miles from the sea, transported over power dams, reaching the spawning beds and surviving into the following sumer, only to be caught. Most kelts die naturally, but couldn't this one have made it back to the sea, if only for poetry's sake? Ecologically, the loss of this spent salmon was nothing to worry about. It had spawned. But I wasn't thinking about it ecologically. I just felt sorry for it, because I identified with it. It should have died hereafter.

I have two postscripts to the trip to the Luttojoki and the Murra-varrakkajoki. The first is that I was called to a conference in Scotland two years later to advise on the installation of a Borland salmon pass at the main dam on the Russian side, which would allow salmon to reach the Luttojoki headwaters and spawn there. The Finns were tendering for the contract. I do not know whether they won it or not, but I was delighted to hear of concern being expressed for the future of salmon in the system and of roubles being spent to improve spawning.

The second postscript is different. I returned to Helsinki and the day after I got there, there was a commotion in one of the main streets. I asked what it was. I was told that an elk had run into the centre of the town and was dislocating the traffic. Then I saw it, a great antlered animal running bewildered between the cars. It had been maddened by flies, an onlooker said and had blundered from the woods into the city. They sometimes did this. They were silly brutes in the summer, some-one said. No one could have gauged the depth of irony that sighting of an unromantic elk had for me. It was my only sighting of an elk in Europe. It was ludicrous. The gods of the Lapland forest had noted my longing and were having a good laugh at my expense.

CHAPTER
14

In the woods of Maine

THE NORTHERN WOODS OF MAINE are usually thought of from New York or Boston as part of a kind of northern paradise where the Appalachian Mountains end in chains of forested hills with myriads of lakes and rivers and ponds, reaching to the frontier with Quebec. I was, however, in my years in North America, based in Montreal and found my longings for the woods of Maine a southern one. They were my idea of escape from a Quebec where there were many polluted rivers, where there was overfishing in the accessible waters and a less than convincing attitude to conservation and protection of the wilderness in the minds of the average citizen. Maine was, for me, the greener field over the fence. From the province of Quebec I was able to enter Maine by one of several back doors, easily reaching the remotest northern woods of the state which my counterparts in Boston might have striven to reach as if they were Ultima Thule.

One such back door was the US State Highway 201, which takes one down from Quebec city through Jackman and Caratunk to the Kennebec River valley. This area is one of fine hilly, wooded country, where forestry is the key to all aspects of the landscape and the community. Pine and mixed deciduous forests clothe every hill and hug every road. Trees are the undisputed masters. Indeed, the forests often prevent you from fishing, because they are virtually imprenetrable, but where they are worked, many have networks of access roads, dirt tracks through the mass of trees which open up the territory to fishers and campers. Some of the forestry companies allow public entry to these road systems for a fee, giving you a map to their forest roads, identifying campsites, forestry offices and houses where there is assistance, issuing the visitor with rules but above all, mapping the rivers and ponds where fishing is to be had and indicating what sport might be expected.

These areas are often huge, the size of British counties and once out on
to the dirt roads of these woods you are quickly into peaceful remote
forests, with natural streams and lakes and ponds where fishing is
hunting, in a way which we in Britain have almost forgotten. In the
woods of Maine, it is one thing to find the river you want hidden in
hundreds of square miles of trees. It is then another quest to explore it,
find where it is fishable, find what it contains and use your skills in
catching the quarry discovered.

My son Mark and I were interested in brook trout *salmo salvelinus
fontinalis*, the char with a string of names like beads on a necklace –
brook trout, eastern brook trout, speckled trout, *truite moucheté*, square-
tails, and where they go into the estuaries and into the sea, sea trout.
I had to adjust at first to 'trout' being used universally to describe a fish
which, in my vocabulary was not a trout at all, but a char. I had to get
used to *my* trout, *salmo trutta*, which all reasonable people throughout
my life had just called 'trout', being given other names in America.
What I might have called in Scotland 'brown trout' or poetically in the
countryside in Ayrshire, 'yellow trout' were, I thought, slightly
disgraced in America by being called 'grey trout'. It was like the sense
of wrongness I felt when, as an Ayrshire Scot, I discovered that, in
England, 'corn' meant wheat and not oats. Worse still, in America and
Canada, 'corn' means maize. You might have expected this feeling of
trout being misnamed to wear off, but the curious thing was that it
never did. There was a real trout in my head, as it were, and it sulked
a bit because its name was misused.

The eastern brook trout are fascinating fish, close relatives of the
salvelinus (char) of deep Scottish lochs and of the rivers and lakes of
Lapland. They do not need to masquerade as any other fish, or borrow
names. They are usually not large fish, but they are eminently worth
hunting for and are very sporting. The largest I caught in my many
fishing trips searching for them in Quebec, New York State, Vermont,
New Hampshire and Maine was a pound-and-a-quarter. My son caught
a fish of just under two pounds in the Canadian Miramichi estuary at
the head of the tide, which was some twelve miles above the actual
mouth of the river. Like any other angler with imagination, I think
I have lost fish which might have been two pounds in weight, but in
two years of searching for brookies of quality I seldom felt confident
that many of that size existed. Once in Quebec, in a river in the Parc de
Joliette, which I had fished unsuccessfully all day, I sat down disconsolately on a stone, almost as the exiles in Babylon might have, hanging
their harps on the willows and weeping for Jerusalem, when I happened
to look down into the stream at my feet and saw a most impressive
speckled brook trout, perhaps three pounds in weight. The sight
immobilised me. If I moved, it would go. I couldn't fish for it without

moving, so I just stared. It was one of these moments in nature when you are given a glimpse of the elusive and the beautiful and the glimpse will last as long as you do not speak or move. I embraced that rare fish with my eyes and, as if it had paraded itself long enough, it suddenly stopped being an exhibit, quickened, turned and swam out of the shallow side stream at my feet and returned to the main river.

I fished in Maine largely in ponds. Do not be deluded by the name. Ponds can often be substantial lakes with long drifts and bays and islands. In some areas it is obligatory to hire a fishing guide. It is also advisable. Ponds can be eight, ten or more miles away up rough forest roads where only competent four-wheel drive vehicles can go. On my first visit to a Maine pond, I hired a local guide, a retired banker, a knowledgeable fisher and in his large jeep we undertook an eight-mile lurch through the woods to a pond near West Forks in Maine one June afternoon and evening. We were half-way there when we turned a bend and found ourselves face to face with a cow moose, standing looking stupid with her long face almost hidden in a cloud of pestering flies. She moved only with reluctance. Indeed, had she not moved, we would not have been able to pass. She was a massive animal, a mountain of deer, blocking the track we were following. That first pond was an education. The brookies were difficult. Scottish loch trout would have been easy meat beside them. I drifted the favoured areas two or three times before I moved fish, and even then failed to hook any brook trout on my nymphs. There was the odd 'shiner' or two – little whitfish-like sprats which would obligingly rise to the flies from time to time. They raised hopes, but fulfilled nothing, as parr do when they play at being wetters and pull your dry fly down. Then, as the evening arrived, I did hook one, a lovely fish of over one pound. That first brookie – one of my best – pulled as hard as any fresh sea trout, but pulled longer. It came fighting to the net. Its capture marked the beginning of a new chapter in my fishing and a new respect for the brook trout. Indeed I would say this. If only Canadian and American fisheries could produce more brookies of that size and quality, they would be a superb sporting resource. In two years of fishing on both sides of the eastern Canadian border, I saw more fish of six inches and less than larger. I fished many waters potentially good habitats for brook trout and found them empty, or emptied. The brookies I found in ponds and rivers were quirky, difficult fish, reluctant to be deceived and hard to hook and bring to the net, but a spendid fishing quarry. If only there were more pounders!

When I did find ponds with better fish in them, they tested all my skills as a fly fisher. For example, in a pond deep in the woods beyond Caratunk, I came across a party of anglers living in a couple of cabins on the bank and they invited me to try my fly for the brook trout that evening, using one of their canoes. The fish, they said, were being difficult. They were feeding hard in the evenings on midges and they could hardly induce any to come to their wet or dry flies. It was, for me, a well-known problem. Scottish trout would act like this in June and July, feeding on what looked like midge soup in the surface film and rejecting all our artificial flies, even the tiniest imitations. I was keen to see whether the evening hatches produced smuts like the little *caenis*, the anglers' curse, or whether the hatch was of the tiny blood-worms which produce the Scottish midge. As the light dimmed, the fish began to rise, not with popping, nicely circled rises, but making little waves and lumps on the fading ripple as they toured and sucked in the hatching flies. They reminded me of 'whispering' rainbows, vacuuming midge nymphs in as they tour in erratic feeding circuits. The midges were in fact buzzers in this case, tiny little ribbed worms. I had in my box some small Footballer nymphs dressed to match the hatching buzzers which we get on English reservoirs and some Scottish lochs in early summer at dusk. I would have expected to pop a Foot-baller in on light tackle in front of a moving fish and give it a twitch to attract the trout. The pond brookies ignored this. I tried larger flies. They ignored me again. Then using the smallest Footballers I had, tiny little shanks ribbed with black and grey horsehair and practically no other dressing, I tried stroking the water with the nymphs with two on a long, fine cast. I had a follow, then a take and for about half an hour I caught and returned fish which ran in size from four to about twelve ounces. They were delightful fish to stalk, and catch. Part of the art was gliding in in the canoe, then sitting still while casting to prevent ripples. Stalking and casting in this way, I found I could go on taking fish in water which became almost glassy calm. Brook trout, in my experi-ence, feed well while there is light and stop rising like rainbows, as soon as the dusk deepens. Brown trout would go on into the dark, feeding with those tantalising plops which are so difficult to locate, and pulling on the wet fly long after the light has faded to the deepest gloom.

It was in Maine that I allowed myself to be seduced by suckers. I came across a group of large fish, looking like mullet, hovering in a pool in a forest stream I had been searching for six-inch or better brookies all day and had nothing. Here were feeding fish, foraging on the bottom and occasionally moving aside to take food coming down with the stream. I half convinced myself that they were grayling at first, but the idea was a hope only. They were more like the large whitefish I had seen in Lapland, but they had the down-turned mouths of mullet. In my fishless state they were a sudden, electrifying focus. I resolved to catch them. I would, moreover, catch them on a fly. I crept up to the pool and popped in a small nymph and the fish paid absolutely no attention to it. The nymph parted the shoal and they seemed neither afraid of it nor attracted to it. It was an irrelevance. I crept round above them and fished a wet fly. They seemed blind to its charms. I left the fish for a while then tried dry fly. I might as well have been fishing in my bath. The shadowy forms, large, fat, attractive, several pounds in weight, went on hoovering the stones of the pool and turning aside to take miniscule items brought down by the stream. They were absolutely impervious to all my skills. I should have let experience guide me. They were in the same clan as the mullet in Brittany which eluded me maddeningly for a fortnight, or those of the Aegean Sea which so spurned me that I took a snorkel and went down to look closely at them. They were sucking the stones, syphoning sea water through their filters and, I swear, were licking the green off the rocks. In the woods of Maine, it must have been troutlessness which made me forget that suckers are not human, as it were. They do not know the joys of rising to a well-presented fly, nor the consummation which comes after a good fight and they are knocked on the head and held up as a trophy for other anglers to see. They are the unregenerate among fish. Pity them; they know not the delights of being caught by anglers. Perhaps we should send in the missionaries. I left these suckers, chastened by their indifference. It was however, nearly time to return to camp and make a meal. I could sit by the barbecue beside my Volvo in the clearing, and let the benison of food take over. I could even hope for proper fish to rise to my flies in the evening.

I did not do well on the streams of the forest. There were odd brookies here and there, of course, but it may well be that I was looking for the fish in lies characteristic of brown trout. I searched streams and tried glides, rushes at the heads of pools and the deep pools themselves. These sudden small deep pools were a surprise to me. Even on small Maine streams one would suddenly find pools several feet deep. In Scotland, you might find occasional deep pools among rocks, or below falls, but generally the hard bedrock and the lack of soil produces a fast, shallow stream. In Maine and elsewhere in New England, streams scour out the soil among the tree roots and produce holts and hides for brookies which are both hard to fish with fly and potentially disastrous to play fish in. It was in Maine that I added the term 'fishing hole' to my vocabulary. In local shops in the small towns people would say that Bobby or Billy knew where the best fishing holes were and I should see them. I thought at first, 'What a horrible term!' and I imagined stagnant pools or dubs, fit only for the worm. I was right and wrong in this. I was wrong in that the holes I found were far from stagnant. Many were turbulent, fast, streamy. I think I was right, however, to think of such places as best suited to worming. I could imagine that the only way to get a fish out of such a deep mass of tree roots would be to yank it out on a worm. I shrank at the thought. My late friend Moray McLaren's words came back to me: 'I am like a lily of the field,' he said, 'I worm not neither do I spin!'. The humour in that saved it from being priggish. I would, in certain circumstances, be a boy again and worm a trout out of a difficult hole. I would also in unusual and extreme cases, such as trying for a massive trout in Lapland, occasionally spin. But having said that, it would no more enter my head to go trout fishing in the woods of Maine with a spinning rod or a bait rod than it would occur to me to harness a racehorse to a cart. It occurs to me that I had better watch my metaphors here. In New England, they do harness racehorses to kinds of cart – to buggies – and they race them. Well, all right. I am prejudiced about fishing. I admit that I would normally rather be fishless than worm out of a forest stream something as deft and darting and subtle as a brook trout. It is prejudice, or rather expectation, which makes me feel this way. I go into the woods or the wilderness expecting to fish with fly, because that is where my pleasure lies. I do not go into the backwoods to be a hunter–gatherer. I treasure the brookies I have caught, even if they have often been small. Perhaps a whole corps of Maine anglers, reading this, will chuckle in unison and marvel that I failed to worm out, subtly, two-, three- and even four-pounders from the holes in the forest streams.

Camping in the woods of Maine and exploring the network of streams and ponds is a perfect example of fishing being about very much more than catching fish. It is about paths through the woods, and vistas through the trees to corner pools on clear waters. It is suddenly seeing ponds, each sighting feeling like discovery. I went into the woods of Maine already in thrall to Robert Frost who lived out his gentle, reflective life in the woods of New England. I do not know if he came as far north as Caratunk in Maine, but his writing embraced it. He said about his poetry something which I think absolutely characterises fishing. It 'begins in delight and ends in wisdom'. Following a Maine stream through the trees and happening on ponds is exactly like that. It is a boyish pursuit, a hopeful joyful adventure with layer upon layer of experience building in you as you progress. The experiences accumulate and form an atmosphere and in this there are moments when one feels quite profoundly moved by places, and encounters with water and fish. It would be crude to take the experiences and insights of the streams and the woods and lay them, like a template, on the rest of life, but there is a subtle exchange between experiences in the woods and what we are elsewhere. We are modified by forests, and by the waters we fish in them. I cannot claim to have felt the wisdom of things as deeply as Frost, but I have felt him with me often as I fished. I feel his love mixed with sadness and unease for places like the woods of

Maine, full of choices of path, changes of colour, moments of awe and obligation mixed. In the endless forests of Maine and in other solitary, fishing places elsewhere, I have felt his lines strongly:

> The woods are lovely, dark and deep,
> But I have promises to keep,
> And miles to go before I sleep,
> And miles to go before I sleep.

Fishing is a privileged way of learning this, a way of identifying with the forest and the northern woods of Maine are the perfect environment for this.

CHAPTER
15

Alaska: the last wilderness

WHAT TAKES A FLY FISHER TO ALASKA is the vastness of the place, its spectacular geography, its lore, its wildness and its abundance of fish. But a visit to Alaska is often infused with a curious irony. It is impossible to go there without being infected in some way by notions of adventure, reverberations of the gold rush, *Boy's Own Paper* adventures, or Alaska's more recent literature and films. Equally, because it is a fierce but lovely wilderness accessible to and part of the United States, it is virtually impossible to go fishing there without meshing with organised tourism – with the established outfitters, or fishing lodges, with guides and access to the interior by small float planes. It is also pretty well impossible not to find that much of your fishing is packaged with a peculiarly American view of the sport, often involving a kind of boyishness. Going to Alaska in this organised way may well be ironic, but when you arrive, the place itself is overwhelming, virtually untamed, primeval and magnificent. Its stunning landscapes and amazing wilderness fecundity transcends all the hype and sweeps the gloss away.

In my case all sorts of romantic anomalies were apparent. I harboured from boyhood a pioneer fishing urge to go to Alaska, derived I think from the *Boy's Own Paper*. In my student days when I first fished in Lapland I talked much about going to the greater wilderness in Alaska, as a climber might plan to ascend higher peaks. It was usually couched in terms of 'Walking down the Yukon, fishing as we go'. How naive! As if that two-and-a-half-thousand-mile river was somehow like a Highland glen. When the chance came to visit Alaska more than thirty years later, it was not to visit the Yukon, however. It came in the form of an attractive invitation from Country Pursuits in Scotland to lead a small group of fishers on an Alaskan fishing week in the prolific Bristol

Bay area. That alluring invitation brought Alaska into focus. It certainly fed on old dreams, but it brought, at last, realistic contact. That extraordinary first week was suffused with experience, and was full of extraordinary fishing. There were also traces of my schoolboy adventure reading. We did, in fact, meet bears and moose and eagles and our fishing guide did carry a forty-five revolver which I had, at one point the great pleasure (and irony) of firing out over a still pool of the Peace River. Alaska thrust at me a compressed seven days, whose real riches only became apparent later in reflection. It was a week of fishing, some of which has made me revise, or at least reconsider, not only the way I fish in gentler landscapes but also how I think about the wilderness itself.

We were, I suppose, typical of many whose journey to the stunning wilderness of Alaska begins with comfortable flights floating over snow-capped mountains set in ridge after ridge below us. We travelled deceptively easily over this vast territory, over the virtually unknown northern interior, over the massive Yukon of boyhood dreams, then down to Anchorage. Below us, where we got a glimpse through the cloud, icy peaks up to 20,000 feet looked benign. At 600 miles per hour, the colossal size and majesty of the place could easily be lost on the traveller. One might doze through a journey which, until our own times would have demanded months, if not years, of unthinkable privations.

From the angler's point of view, Alaska is undoubtedly one of the last great fishing wildernesses of the world. It is still absolutely awe-inspiring. It is a realm of the most dauntingly large, elemental rivers and lakes, of vast resources of fish, of beavers and bears, moose and eagles. From July to the middle of September its ice and snows recede and the whole vast state, the size of Europe, seems to relax, open its doors, and welcome the visiting angler. It does welcome you, but I was most impressed in the August I visited Alaska with the first briefing of our host, Burt Bomhoff, in the fishing lodge in the interior above Bristol Bay. There we were, having flown from London to Anchorage, flown again to Dillingham, having been picked up in a fleet of small float planes and flown yet another sixty miles inland to the lodge – a most comfortable cluster of log houses by the shores of a remote and stunningly beautiful lake. 'Alaska is a most beautiful fishing wilderness', he said, 'But it is also a most unforgiving place'. The relevance of this took me back to weeks out on the tundra of Lapland. It centred on one image. We were miles out in a sparse forest with no sign of habitation, yet from time to time wooden skis were to be found propped against trees. When I asked my companion what they were for he said that the Lapps left them there because, caught in a sudden storm, these skis would save your life. Alaska, in a much more dramatic and

potentially harsh landscape, was teaching the same message. It was
teaching that, like all wildernesses, it had a corollary to its solace and
beauty. It would annihilate those who treated it thoughtlessly. To bring
reality home with a bump, the weather on our arrival at Golden Horn
Lodge was foul – low cloud, wind and prolonged heavy rain. Our three
single-engined Beavers and a Cessna lurched their way through valleys
where clouds met the tree tops. Landing at Michalk Lake and taxi-ing
to the landing stage at Golden Horn was welcome. We unloaded, in the
mirk, drank some tea and were immediately taken to try for char where
a pounding, flooded river flowed into our home lake. It was entirely
fitting that, in our hasty fishing of the cold wet flood we found there,
none of us took anything that evening.

During the night the three-day rain stopped. When the sun rose that
first clear morning, the landscape it revealed was breathtaking. Our
cluster of log houses sat on the eastern shores of the charming small
Michalk Lake, tucked into the lakeside pines which rose steeply into
scrub behind and reached the tree line about 500 feet above us. A mile or
so to the north of the camp a powerful, clear river poured in, the Wind
River. Draining the lower end of the lake half a mile below us was the
wide, gentler, Peace River. Both were part of the substantial Wood
River complex which, sixty or so miles below, reached Dillingham and
joined the vast Nushagac estuary just above the point at which it flows
into Bristol Bay. This bay is a prolific focus for Pacific salmon runs and
in the short and hectic fishing season which the summer in Alaska
allows, Bristol Bay brings salmon in by the million to run the rivers
and fill the lakes above.

Salmon fishers with an Atlantic salmon background may find the
Pacific salmon scene extraordinary. When we arrived in late August we
were just in time for the runs of silver salmon (coho), the most sought
after quarry of the fly fisher. In the rivers and lakes we fished, there
were millions of very red, spawning sockeye. Some reaches of rivers
were coloured red, so dense were the ranks of hundreds of thousands of
the fish. From the air, some lake bays were seen to be packed with
sockeye, obscuring the bottom. Some of the smaller creeks we waded
were littered with the dead and dying bodies of sockeye. In the third
week of August, we were too late for the chum salmon. Their short
run was already over and there was no trace of their large runs in any
of the rivers we fished. We were very much too late for the king
salmon (chinook), the largest of the Alaskan salmon which runs in June
and July. In the six weeks or so since their coming had filled the larger
rivers with thirty-, forty- and fifty-pounders, they had coloured,
spawned and died. Without going further into other migratory fish, nor
into local races, this astonishing Alaskan resource of migratory fish can
only be regarded as mind-numbing. It is hard to grasp the huge size of

the runs, the atavistic brevity of the river sojourn, the rapid maturation, the spawning and death. For those used to Atlantic salmon, to meet a prolific and hectic migratory spawning scene like that in Alaska, is just too fast-forward a picture to be grasped. Not just one run of vast numbers, but run after run come in, many forging incredibly far inland, rushing to the spawning grounds, spawning, layer upon layer – millions pelting headlong to reproduction and death.

Yet, in a short time it became commonplace to wade creeks while dry fly fishing for grayling or looking for rainbows to nudge aside the sockeye lying in the streams. Some of the sockeye were not past fishing for and would still take a fly, often quite vigorously. One afternoon, finding our first choice of river in flood, we fished for red sockeye in a packed stream joining Lake Nekra to Lake Aleknagik. We chose this water in an interesting way. We flew round the shores of the lake, looking for massed fish. We spurned bays with 500 or a 1,000, but decided to try the river I describe which had probably 3,000 fish lying in its shingly estuary. I waded and found these shoaled sockeye easing back from me like sheep. Now and again a red cock sockeye would barge at my legs, thinking I was a spawning intruder. All five of our group fished there for an hour or so and I think I am right in saying that I saw all five rods into fish at the same time. It was, of course, a new experience for us, but I found, before the hour was up, I was beginning to hunt for the wild rainbows which had joined the sockeye, to feed on the eggs they were about to shed. Even casting the smaller fly, however, I still hooked sockeye in that bay of plenty.

This prolific scene has its macabre side too. On the attractive upper reaches of the Nushagak River half an hour's flying to the east of the lodge, we fished for Alaskan wild rainbows. The fly was tied with trailing white rabbit fur – an enormous creation on a great single hook. That fly was said to represent the flesh of dead sockeye salmon, on which big rainbows feed. We fished the snaggy lies – sunk branches, waterlogged trees, working the White Rabbit out from the underwater tangle of twigs. The guide said corpses of sockeye hung there, providing food for the rainbows. We caught them, and there were some nice rainbows among them, up to four pounds. I tell myself that I should feel content that the death of one fish should feed the life of another, but, at that particular time, the White Rabbit and the technique of the snags seemed rather squeamish facts which pushed the profligacy of Alaska over the top into grossness.

We timed our visit well for a whole range of fish. Firstly, we discovered the char in the lakes, gathering for their spawning run up feeder streams. One little bay behind an island with a burn flowing in took my fancy. I fished a size six single red bodied hairwing which I had tied up specially for the day. I had great sport with fish of two,

three and more pounds. They pulled at the fly like big trout and they
pulsed into the lake as they fought. I was thigh deep in that reach when
I saw what looked like a yard of goldfish swim past – a sockeye cock.
I was casting for my char, landing the fly under the trees and drawing it
off when the bar of gold appeared again, suddenly changed direction
and a second later I had the pull indicating that the fish had taken my
char fly. It tore off out into the lake and ran harder than any of the other
sockeye I had hooked that week. When it came into the net, it was an
astonishing fish, bright red with an olive green head, a huge hump back
and a tail flecked with bright golden patches. It was about fourteen
pounds, big for a sockeye. The boatman and I looked down at it, a
massive goldfish with a green head and jaws festooned with teeth like
something malicious from the Amazon. It was beautiful and ugly at the
same time. The boatman said, 'I would love to trophy that!' – which,
being interpreted means that he would like to have the fish to set it up.
'By all means', I said, stooping down to take out the fly. The fish at
that moment turned and snapped at me like a terrier, drawing blood
from my thumb. 'I think he heard us', said the boatman.

Each day we flew to a different lake or river. Our effective range was
about sixty miles from the lodge. One day it would be fishing a flooded
river flowing into Nuyakuk Lake. Another would take us to the attractive Agulapak river, full of red salmon and rainbows. I found much of
it extraordinary. On one stream flooding into a lake, we fished flies tied
to represent salmon eggs, quaint little balls like pink peas. Another fly,
a Woolly Bugger, was tied up in two-inch streamer-form to represent a
lamprey with an egg in its mouth. It was a fly fishing scene different
from anything I had known before, although obviously related to lure
fishing for rainbows at home. Sometimes there was clear logic in it,
even if the flies were not flies at all. I felt myself becoming very keen on
this wilderness fly fishing, because it could range all the way from the
finest of dry fly sport with large grayling to streamer and other deep
lure fishing for rainbows. What I found a little difficult to accept, at
times, was a kind of over-enthusiasm for catches. Sometimes the whole
operation went over the top into a 'get them at any price' mentality.
For instance, in the lower pools of a small river feeding a large lake
I had fished an egg fly and had two large grayling in a fast run and was
quite content. The guide disappeared and I later saw him spooning
something out of a tin into the river about two hundred yards above
me. I thought he was wantonly disposing of some rubbish and I was
angry. In fact he was 'chumming' – putting salmon eggs into the stream
to bring fish up from the lake. Horrors! What would they say in the Fly
Fishing Club! When I spoke to him about it and said that ground
baiting to keep my rod bending actually diminished my fun, I think he
believed he had come across old world eccentricity.

We shared some waters with others from the lodge, and they included the staff of a Las Vegas casino. There they were, the Big Boss, the minders, the floor managers, the pilot of the private jet and the guests. They were having the time of their lives, mostly spinning, much of which was done with a boyish glee, grinding away with their spinning reels as if they were expecting a jackpot. They waded out into the lake, forming a line and covered the water sweetened by the flood as it flowed into the deep cold stillwater. There were fish of some quality there and some way along the shore. One of our party took a five pound lake trout (a char); others took grayling and smaller char. The casino men were interesting and unusual companions, but I felt that I wanted to wander off and and try other pools, other creeks. So, watching for grizzly bears, whose footprints were often plain on the sand of the lakeshore, I wandered off, fished the lake like a Scottish loch and raised nothing, found a little creek where some sockeye splashed, found fresh tracks of a massive bear and moose, and came back, fishless but feeling I had seen and felt something of the place. When I arrived back, the bonanza fishing was still going on at the mouth of the flooded feeder. A rod-bending spree was in full swing; the guide was chumming away with his salmon eggs. It was, of course, a delightful scene, full of human happiness. Returning to the serious business of fly fishing, however, we spoke to our pilot and he did that lovely, free, Alaskan thing – he loaded us into our beaver and flew us to another place where we were alone with a few thousand salmon, some interesting rainbows and our own peculiar fly-fishing goals.

We longed for silver salmon that week, but the weather pinned us down. Low cloud and mist prevented us going on schedule to the Togiak River, to our west. Instead we fished rivers and creeks north and east of the lodge, often trying two different waters in a day. We caught grayling and char, wild rainbows, sockeye and finally silvers. The first of them came from a gentle pool where a creek joined the Nushagak River. The first two silvers were coloured, rose pink, attractively shaped, keen takers and hard pullers. These Nushagak fish were from the earliest runs which were now well upstream. They had coloured rapidly, perhaps in a week, and were excellent fish to take, but their rose flanks belied their silver name. We hoped that they were the harbingers of fresher fish to be taken later in the week when the weather cleared and we could get to the lower Togiak. There we would catch silver silvers, straight from the sea. But the mist persisted until Wednesday when the first party from the lodge made it to the Togiak, where they spun its high water and had instant success. Our turn was to come the following day, and we fretted as we waited for the morning mist to lift and for the clouds to be pronounced high enough for the Beaver to cross the pass and get us to the Togiak. Eventually it did, and we eased through the pass under the low cloud and saw the lower Togiak, shining in its flooded plain, full of islands, distributaries and backwaters.

The Togiak is a fascinating river, cold, greenish, with strong streams over gravel. Here and there the shingle forms islands, some no more than temporary heaps of gravel, some bound by shrubs and small trees into something more permanent. The gravel, which was to prove vital to our fishing, also forms spits and headlands and those haaf-like bars parallel to the bank which enclose sheltered water known as 'slues' (a variant form of 'slough'). The wadeable gravel and the slues were to be most important for us, partly for good fishing reason, in that they affected the pattern of running and pausing of the silvers, but partly for a curious, bad reason connected with access to the banks proper. The slues were the main holding lies and they were fascinating. Gravel bars parallel to the bank would enclose water fishable from the gravel, or nicely wadable. The larger slues also offered gentle water which was fishable from the boat. These sheltered reaches were clear at knee deep and progressively darker green as they slid down into deeper holes, some providing access to lies under the bushy banks, which would have been unfishable from the bank itself.

When we met our boatmen there, we were briefed that we could use our boats to travel, and we could fish from them or wade, but we must not land on the bank. Even if we had not been told, the notices every twenty yards or so facing the river informed us that the banks were the property of the local people and landing was forbidden. It was an extremely strange situation to find a river where we had the right to fish, but not to fish from the banks. Apparently, the Indigenous Peoples Land Act made land available to local Indian and Eskimo residents and in the case of some of the salmon rivers, the local people, Eskimos (Inuit) and Indians, played a crafty card. They opted to take their acreage in a narrow strip up the sides of salmon rivers. The move, designed to exclude landing and camping, partly succeeded, but float planes were able to land, and navigation was still permitted. Since the bank has a legal definition, all the exposed bed of the river, its islands, its gravel bars, islands and all its wadeable area was accessible. Camping was possible on the shingle banks and spits and some quite large tented fishing camps were set up on shingle islands which, in a very large flood, might well be in danger of being washed off. It was comic opera stuff to find a river in the wilderness where one could legally fish, but not have access to the banks. Most bizarre of all, the local people, while still not allowing bank access, entered into letting agreements for the fishing. Indeed, they ran camps there for visitors. The Togiak was itself a marvellous wilderness river but the bizarre access arrangements and the anomalies of its operation seem to me to reveal a prospect 'where every aspect pleases and only man is vile'.

The day begins with hunting for the right slues. We cruised downstream, tried the mouth of a small creek for ten minutes, then a stream of the main river, before we spotted what we wanted to see, a slue with fish showing. We were three rods in that boat, Jim Fisher from Glasgow, an expert salmon fisher, Malcolm Scott from Edinburgh and myself. The gravel spit was restricted, so, in Alaskan style, we fished twenty yards apart, casting straight into the sheltered water. Jim hooked a fish immediately and produced after a fast fight our first clean silver, about seven pounds, beautifully shaped, silvery with a hint of green at the head, and at first sight, very like an Atlantic salmon except for the shape of the jaws and head. I pulled one and Jim took a second on his size two black hairwing with 'flashaboo' mixed in. The silvers were said to want gaudy flies. They were also said to want well-sunk flies, but we did not find that. A sink tip would have done it. We were, of course, fishing single-handed carbon rods there, eleven-footers or thereabouts, good sea trout items. I lamented the lack of my fifteen-footer. It was not that fighting the fish was too hard on the small rod; it was the casting which was troublesome. In restricted places, say when you are wading down with a tree-lined bank behind you, it is a spey cast you want. Above all, it is a fifteen-foot carbon salmon rod you crave for. The longer rod also has greater casting range. Several times during my fishing of the Togiak, I found myself wading deeper than I might have wished, just to reach a likely bit of water or achieve casting space behind. I also missed the rhythm of the long rod, so conducive to good salmon fishing. With the shorter rod you are in a different gear. Further, the difficulties it brings in long casting means that you have to go through the performance of false casting with double hauling, trying to accelerate the line enough to reach showing fish. That can make you look like a lunatic who has just discovered semaphore.

My first silver was a cracker. We had moved down to another slue and this time we found that wading would not allow us to reach the showing fish, which were in a deep hole under the bushes. We persuaded the boatman to take us one by one into the area, holding off to allow proper covering of the lie. He had very poor oars and we had to improvise rowlocks. It is typical of Alaska that boats have wonderful, even elaborate, outboard motors and they seem to assert that the age of the oar is over. Heaven knows what would happen if a serious bit of survival-rowing had to be undertaken.

Each rod in that productive slue had the chance to fish under the trees and on hooking a salmon, the boat was drawn back and the lie left more or less undisturbed. It was alive with fish. All three of us took fish there. My first silver, a good thirteen-pounder with a high back, drew the fly nicely like a salmon at home, then did things no Scottish

salmon has ever heard of. First it ran in a great semi-circle below the
boat then turned sharply, like a great rainbow, and ran in a series of
short fast arcs making the line hiss through the water as the reel gave
line in short high pitched-bursts. That silver seemed to me to be more
powerful than an Atlantic salmon of similar size, but it is hard to tell.
Our salmon run, usually, in straight lines. They pulse and pause and
pull hard before running again out into the stream. Silver salmon
scutter all over the place at high speed. They show at the surface and
jump or half-jump and indulge in 'tail walking' in a way I have only
seen before in rainbows. They are marvellous sporting fish and, as far
as I could judge, are free takers. The Togiak was brilliantly living up to
its reputation.

We met the other boat for lunch. We laid six fish out for the morning; Tim and John had had seven between them in a great burst of
sport, fishing off a shingle bar. The morning had been magnificent.
Every rod had had fish. The air was thick with stories and speculation
about the afternoon. We ate quickly, changed boats and boatmen and
set off to play the Togiak game again.

The afternoon that day showed the fitfulness of silver salmon fishing.
In a creek, I got one and pulled another, but that was the end of any
contact with fish. We scurried up river, visited places which had been
full of salmon in the morning and, although we occasionally saw a fish
splashing, none of us touched any. Was it just one run of fish which had
gone through? Were the fish still there but, for some atmospheric
reason, had become dour? I think the lower reaches of the Togiak really
only fish well when salmon are running. They do not seem to hold
resident fish. Of course, runs are regular and species are varied and
there may well always be fish to catch, give or take pauses of a few
hours. For example, we were asked at the lodge on our return if we had
taken any Dolly Varden, the sea-going char. The fact that we had not
caused a little surprise. My strong suspicions that we had just managed
to cover the tail end of a substantial run of silvers was confirmed when
a small party of our Las Vegas friends flew the following day to the
upper Togiak, where our lodge did not have a boat and where wading
was said to be impossible. They spun from the floats of the plane, and
again were into silvers all day. The speed of runs in Alaska is stunning.
In Scotland we sometimes say salmon can run upstream on average as
fast as you could walk up beside them on the bank. In Alaska they seem
to ascend as if they were motor-assisted.

One of the special features of our fishing area, out from Golden Horn
Lodge, was a wild rainbow fishery of some quality. West of the lodge,
a lake on the upper part of a small river, the Negulthlik, held, it was
claimed, the best wild rainbows anywhere. The lake was fed by a small
deep, weedy stream which wound circuitously among rushes and moss.

The river flowing out of the lake below was similar, but had more pools and streams in its character. We landed on the lake and divided into two parties, three rods, of which I was one, fishing the mossy upper feeder and two fishing the lower river. We were briefed – all fish to be returned without excessive handling, barbless hooks, no wading. The technique advocated was, fish big, fish sunk, fish slow. The guide urged me to tie on a 2/0 Woolly Bugger, which was so heavy my eleven-foot heavy-duty rod could hardly cast it. I changed to a slightly smaller Muddler Minnow, but again I was hard pressed not to hit myself on the head with this massive object being pulled back and forth on the air in casting. It was an open stream through grassy moor and it was a small and clear one. Therefore we had to keep well out of sight. If you can imagine the difficulties of casting a heavy fly from a crouching position, and making sure you popped in right under the far bank of the creek, you will be sympathetic. I eventually began to get some kind of rhythm into it, but the tackle was very unbalanced for the job.

I was fishing a neutral line with a braided, sinking leader attached to a long cast of eight-pound monofilament. I felt I wanted to move the fly to make fish lying under the far bank pursue the lure. I had several strong follows with waves on the surface, then quite quickly caught two of the largest grayling I have seen since my days in Lapland. The best must have been three-and-a-half pounds. But, even if I had landed grayling, I had the strongest hunch that the powerful marks of pursuit I was seeing on the surface were not grayling, but big rainbows. Some made waves like salmon. I was on my knees working my way down a slow pool when the guide came up and suggested that my fly was too near the surface. He said rainbows never came up for flies drawn off like that. Just at that moment, I had a follow with waves like a torpedo. 'Just a chance fish', he said. I told him to wait and watch and on my way down the pool had two more offers like this. He merely said, 'They've never done that before'. Why was I not catching these fish? Perhaps the rainbows would pursue flies fished up in the water but would have the confidence to take them if sunk just a little deeper. Sea trout are sometimes like that. I was not sure of the argument, however. I decided to try a slightly smaller fly. I immediately stopped getting follows but took a rainbow, not a large fish – somewhere around three pounds and I was busy with this when Jim came down with two amazing pieces of news. First, that he had had a rainbow of ten pounds, a magnificent fish. Then fishing the next run down, he had hooked a fish which he said was two or three pounds heavier. It ran and pulled and then lay in the stream like a great bar of silver. The barbless hook came out towards the end of the fight. Malcolm came down reporting a seven-pounder, then a lull in activity. John and Tim, fishing the river below the lake later reported that they had spotted a fish of enormous

size in the clear water and had spent their whole time offering it flies,
wet, dry, fast and slow, but without effect. These wild Alaskan rainbows, taken from that small canal-like creek feeding the lake were
outstanding fish. The rainbow, taken in its wild state in the mountain
rivers and lakes of America, is a fish of the highest quality. It is
marvellous to fish for, because it is wary and demanding. It is hair-
raising to fight and subdue large rainbows, because of their power and
agility. The stillwater rainbows we breed and release in Britain are
interesting enough fish, but they are mere shadows of these magnificent, wild fish in their Alaskan home waters.

Alaska is such a rich fishing environment that it is almost an affront
to talk about it after only a week. Yet, some of the major fishing events
of my life have lasted for less. One week sampling the enormous
variety of waters and fish in the Bristol Bay area went through a whole
series of phases and raised in a special way many issues which are at the
heart of fishing. The Alaskan experience, for me, began with a degree
of culture shock, and, as we have said, an interesting element of irony.
As I fished, and the richness of the place and its fishing was borne in on
me, I had the impression of compressing into a few days a vast compass
of angling experience. It was several weeks after my return home
before I felt the raw data of Alaska maturing. Some of the confusions of
the week resolved themselves. I found myself seeing through the mass
of it all and appreciating the real riches of fishing there. A longing for
the place grew, in patches at first. One year later, in August, I found
myself wondering, quite passionately, how the Togiak runs were
going. The following year, I read some reports from Alaska and felt a
strong desire to go back. I wanted to see more remote waters, perhaps
much further north, waters where fish might be scarcer, but the
rewards of taking them might be proportionately higher. I have not yet
made the return journey, but the urge is now strong.

I have spoken to other anglers who have fished in Alaskan waters and
they have all spoken of how difficult it is to get your mind round
Alaska and enjoy it fully on first contact. A friend of mine left his
Alaskan fishing after four days, perplexed because he had taken two
thirty-pound-plus king salmon virtually on successive casts and it
disturbed him. Another, having taken a massive king salmon, said it
was wonderful but he kept wishing it had been a fresh sixteen pounder
from the Dee. I think we might call this the Alaskan bounty syn-
drome. Perhaps it hints at an even broader psychological truth. The real
message of the place lies on the other side of the first rather gross blast
of experience. It is almost, for some, as if the truth lay on the other side
of revulsion. Alaska, in my view, is not to be discovered in the fire of
its advertising, nor the whirlwind of its organised fishing. It lies beyond
that in the much quieter, more meaningful voice of the wilderness and

its fragility. When it was being grossly prolific, that wilderness reminded me of the fisher who at first thought that a fish every cast was heaven, before he discovered that he was, in fact, in hell. Alaska, if you get through the heaps and heaps of fish, has many ways of reminding you that fishing is a quest and that wilderness is a privilege rather than a bonanza in a natural playground. It is not until you learn this that the real value of the place comes through. I liked the way Alaska contradicted some of its own advertising. I was very conscious there of rediscovering that perfect fishing pleasure is more difficult to find in a pool holding a quarter-of-a-million salmon than it is on a beat of the Helmsdale in February where a single, unexpected fresh fish can bring Elysian serenity to a blank spring week.

Bibliography

CURRIE, W. B., *Days and Nights of Game Fishing*, Unwin Hyman, 1987
FROST, Robert, *Collected Poems*, 'Stopping by Woods on a Snowy Evening', Pelican Books, n.d.
GRAHAME, Kenneth, *The Wind in the Willows*, Methuen, 1871
GREY Viscount Grey of Fallodon, *Fly Fishing*, Dent, 1899
LAWRENCE, D. H. *Selected Essays* 'Man is a Hunter', Penguin, 1950
SCROPE, William, *Days and Nights of Salmon Fishing*, Murray, 1843
SUTHERLAND, Halliday, *Lapland Journey*, Bles, 1938
WOOD, A. H. E., *Greased-line Fishing*, in *Salmon Fishing*, ed. Taverner, E; Seeley, Service & Co, n.d.

Index